HERBAL

A SIMPLIFIED GUIDE TO
NATURAL HEALTH CARE FOR CHILDREN

BY

STEVEN H. HORNE

WHITMAN BOOKS, INC.
WARSAW, IN 46580

ISBN 10: 1-885653-04-2
ISBN 13: 978-1-885653-04-8

FIRST PRINTING 1992
SECOND PRINTING 1993
THIRD PRINTING 1995
FOURTH PRINTING 1998
FIFTH PRINTING 2005
SIXTH PRINTING 2008

WHITMAN BOOKS, INC.
302 E. WINONA AVENUE
WARSAW, IN 46580
1-800-421-2401

PRINTED IN THE UNITED STATES OF AMERICA

COVER PHOTOGRAPH BY PAT ROBINS
PICTURED ON COVER: KATIE HORNE

ACKNOWLEDGMENTS

Special thanks to Gaylynn Belliston for her assistance in editing and
typesetting this book. Special thanks also to David Skousen and Jo Ann
Bigler for their proofreading assistance.

DISCLAIMER

This book is for educational purposes only. It is not intended to replace
the services of licensed, professional health care providers. Readers are
encouraged to use this material in conjunction with the advice of their
physician.

Table of Contents

Home Remedies

n recent years, many people have returned to relying on herbal home remedies. Numerous books are appearing on the subject. These remedies are commonly referred to as "alternative" health care. This is because most people with health problems go to a licensed, medical doctor first. Then, if they are unable to find relief through this "orthodox" source, they turn to an herbalist, naturopath or massage therapist as an "alternative." Often this is done out of desperation or frustration, rather than informed choice.

In our family, nutrition, herbs and massage are our primary means of health care. We try these simple, natural means first. We find they are especially effective when applied in early stages of disease. Why use the "big guns" of modern crisis medical care on a minor sniffle or a low- grade fever? If the problem is persistant or life-threatening, then of course we need this high-powered professional help. We will seek it, too. But we will not waste our money nor the doctor's time and energy on common ailments which we can safely and effectively treat at home. So in our case, "orthodox" modern medicine is the "alternative." Home remedies are our primary form of health care.

This is the way it was for most of our grandparents and great-grandparents. People used to have their family remedies for common health problems. Unfortunately, this knowledge is largely lost. Many modern parents run their children to the doctor for every minor ailment. Even some doctors realize that this is not good. The family physician we visited when I was a young boy once remarked to my mother, "I don't know why people don't try any home remedies anymore. I've been to see people when I was sicker than they were."

Those who use herbs and other home remedies on themselves are often afraid to treat their own young children. This is partly because parents today lack the "common sense" understanding of things their great-grandparents had. They may be afraid their treatment won't be effective enough and the child may be harmed as a result. They may even fear criminal prosecution by the state should their treatment fail. This is compounded by the fact that most herb books are written primarily for adult problems. There are almost no herb books geared toward herbal remedies for young children.

My wife and I can empathize with these concerns, because we had them when we started taking responsibility for the health care of our own children. However, we are glad that we made the decision to become the primary health care providers for our children. We have been greatly blessed as a result. Our home remedies have proven to be MORE EFFECTIVE than the treatments offered by orthodox medicine for the same complaints.

For example, we can honestly tell you that we have seen sore throats, fevers and earaches gone within a few hours. We've settled stomachs, relieved headaches and taken the pain out of injuries in minutes. Colds and respiratory congestion are usually gone in 24 to 48 hours. In fact, as of this writing, we have four children, and in twelve years, we have only had to take a child to a medical doctor for treatment twice. The first time was nearly eleven years ago when our oldest daughter was one year old. That was before we learned most of the principles taught in this book. Today, we could easily handle the same complaint at home. More recently, one of our boys fell and hurt his neck and we took him to the doctor for x-rays, just to make certain nothing was seriously damaged. We do occasionally take our children to a chiropractor for an adjustment, but other than that we haven't had the need for doctors of any kind.

In contrast, we've listened to many parents tell us about fevers and earaches that lasted for days. We know families where the children are constantly battling colds, respiratory congestion and infections. These families are taking their children to medical doctors for treatment on a regular basis and complying with their instructions. Generally, the doctors give the children antibiotics. The children then develop thrush (yeast infection) which weakens their immune system. Each time they are taken off the antibiotics, they wind up with some other infection, often worse than the one they just "recovered" from. After constant battles with earaches, the children wind up getting tubes in their ears. We've seen eighteen-month-old babies with severe urinary tract infections and pneumonia after ten rounds of antibiotics.

Something is not right here. Compared to ours, these "doctored" children look pasty and pale. Their eyes are not as bright. They are more emotionally stressed. Often they are petrified of strangers because of their experiences with drugs and hospitals. Often the parents feel that something is wrong, but they are afraid to try anything else. If the "big guns" of modern medicine have been unable to help their children, what chance could dietary changes or herbs do? When they try some of our home remedies out of exasperation, they are usually impressed with the rapid, dependable results they obtain.

So, our success is not due simply to the fact that we have been blessed with healthy children. We have been blessed, of course. We acknowledge that our children have been spared thus far from any broken bones or serious lacerations that would definitely require medical care. However, the greater blessing is that we have been given the knowledge we needed to handle the problems on our own, simply and effectively.

We want you to know that we are not fanatical about avoiding doctors. We know that modern medicine is wonderful and necessary for certain serious and life-threatening situations. However, this does not mean we have to discard all the knowledge of the past. Many of the home remedies of the past were and still are tremendously effective.

We must issue you a very important caution, however. We have taken responsibility for the health care of our children. However, we cannot and will not assume the responsibility for the health care of your children. God entrusted our children to us and He entrusted your children to you. So, if you're not willing and able to make intelligent, informed decisions about what you can reasonably handle and what requires professional assistance, don't even try. This book is not intended to replace professional assistance. It is only our way of sharing the knowledge that has richly blessed our family with your family.

The purpose of this book is strictly educational. We can only share our knowledge and experiences with you. If you decide to try any of the remedies in this book on your children, then you must realize that you (not we) are taking the responsiblity for those decisions. You must exercise your own common sense and realize when a situation is beyond your ability to treat. In those circumstances, you should promptly seek appropriate medical attention. We would also suggest that you seek professional help if ailments don't respond to your home remedies in a reasonable amount of time.

We don't want to discourage you from trying, but we do want you to know that every course of action involves some risk. Even taking your child to a doctor involves some risk. It is up to you to weigh the risk and decide what is best for your family. We want to reassure you that it is not difficult to learn to take care of most ailments. In fact, even doctors estimate that we would recover from 70-80% of most ailments if we just rested in bed and drank plenty of fluids. So why not experiment with home remedies for these non-life-threatening illnesses? We are certain you will discover, as we have, that God created the herbs and foods our bodies need to heal themselves. He also made their use simple enough that any person of average intelligence can learn to use them effectively.

May God bless your family with this knowledge as He has ours.

Steven H. Horne, December 1991

PART ONE

The ABC's of Healing

ost herb books give you a list of diseases and the herbs people have used to treat them. These books are useful, but they give you the impression that you must use certain herbs to overcome certain diseases. We have discovered that this is not the case. All diseases have common root causes and all diseases may be treated using the same general principles. By learning and applying these general principles we have actually been able to invent our own home remedies. We have been able to substitute a different herb than the one most people use and still obtain excellent results. Understanding these general principles gives you a flexibility and confidence that no other approach can match. So, the first thing we need to do is lay down the basic principles of natural health care.

HEALTH AND SICKNESS

Through the work of a 19th century herbalist, Samuel Thomson, we have learned to think of the body as a wood stove. Like a stove, our body takes in air and fuel and burns it to create heat or energy. It also has to eliminate the waste products (smoke and ash) from this process. As long as you stoke up the body's fire with good food and air (and lots of love), it will burn clean and hot with a minimum of waste. That means the body will have plenty of energy to run its various functions and the elimination of waste will be satisfactory.

However, if you put cheap fuel (i.e. "junk" food) into the body's firebox, then the fire will burn poorly and the body will become clogged with waste. This will produce a lack of energy to properly run the body's many processes, which will undoubtedly result in disease.

We believe that the symptoms of disease are the result of the body's efforts to remove waste material out of the system. The body has four "chimneys" which it can use for this purpose—the digestive tract, the urinary system, the skin and the respiratory passages. When the body tries to eliminate waste through the digestive tract we experience nausea, vomiting and diarrhea (i.e., the "flu"). When the body uses the skin to eliminate waste we have body odor, rashes, pimples and pox. If the respiratory passages are used to get rid of this material, we will experience runny noses, coughs, earaches, sore throats and other ailments that accompany respiratory congestion. Lastly, the body may also use the kidneys to eliminate unwanted material which can cause kidney and bladder irritations and infections. Fevers are also an effort of the body to "burn up" waste material so it can be more easily eliminated.

If any of the above is the case, the symptoms of the disease are not the enemy. They are the result of the body's efforts to heal itself, to get rid of the disease. In other words, the cold symptoms are the body's way of curing the cold. Anything you do to suppress the cold symptoms only prolongs the length of time it takes for the body to relieve the sickness. This is why doctors have been unable to find a cure for the cold. The cold IS the cure!

Unfortunately, most people think that the symptom *is* the disease. They want something that will suppress the symptoms. Think of this in terms of vomiting. Suppose you just ate something that was tainted and you experience food poisoning. Is the vomiting the sickness? Of course not. The vomiting is the body's way of eliminating the sickness. Hence, it would do no good to suppress the vomiting as this would only prolong your misery and suffering.

Since the symptoms are a result of the body's life processes, the only way to suppress the symptoms is by poisoning the body. This is why most drugs are dilute doses of poisons. These small doses of poison give the appearance of a cure, but they actually interfere with long term health and vitality. This is why the child who is always being taken to the doctor for medications is often more sickly than the child who is not.

Instead of trying to use poisons to suppress disease symptoms, we need to use methods which support the body in its efforts to eliminate the disease. This is done by supplying the body with the same things it required to stay healthy in the first place—nutrition, rest, exercise, love, touch, etc. These methods help strengthen the body so that the body can complete its process of eliminating the disease. In other words, the body will heal itself if we provide it with the conditions and raw materials it needs to affect repairs. This is the great secret of all natural healing.

The Role of Herbs

Some plants are used for food to provide calories for the body to burn. Other plants are poisonous. In between these two extremes lie medicinal herbs. Herbs are not like the plants we eat for calories because we do not consume them in large quantities. They are not poisons either. They are nature's natural nutritional supplements. My herbal mentor, Edward Milo Millet, called them special resource foods. They supply chemical substances in a natural form which the body can use to restore failing functions and repair damaged tissues.

When used with common sense, none of the herbs in this book are dangerous. We have never observed any harm to come from their prudent use. A few of the herbs recommended in this book are controversial because some people feel they may have toxic side-effects. Where this is the case, we have so noted. However, our experience with these plants leads us to believe that they are perfectly safe or we would not use them.

Actions of Herbs

There are only four basic actions of herbs. Herbs either: (1) stimulate body tissues to restore energy when they are sluggish and cold, (2) contract tissues that are loose, spongy or discharging, (3) relax and open tissues that are tense, blocked or obstructed or (4) soothe tissues that are irritated, sore or inflamed.

These qualities can readily be detected by our sense of taste, smell and touch. Herbs which stimulate have aromatic or spicy qualities. They include most of our kitchen spices such as: thyme, peppermint, cayenne pepper (capsicum), rosemary, cinnamon, horseradish, mustard powder, ginger, cloves, oregano and so forth. These spices help to increase the energy of body tissues, improve digestion, expel gas from the bowel, promote perspiration, clear blocked respiratory passages and fight infection. Adults commonly use "hot" aromatics like ginger and cayenne pepper, but children seldom need herbs this strong. Their systems respond very well to pleasantly "sweet" or mild aromatics like: peppermint, spearmint, cinnamon and lemon grass.

Herbs which contract tissues have a sour or astringent (drying and tightening) taste. Think of biting into a lemon and how it puckers your mouth and you will have an excellent idea of what these tightening herbs do. They help to arrest bleeding, stop discharges, reduce swelling, arrest diarrhea, counteract bites and stings and restore tone to flabby organs. Examples of these kinds of herbs include: oak bark, raspberry leaves, bayberry rootbark, yarrow, gumweed, plantain, comfrey and uva ursi. Many berries and fruits have a mild toning action and are very suitable for children such as elderberries and elder flowers, lemon juice, rose hips, blackberries and raspberries.

Those herbs which help to open obstructions in the body, relax tissues, clean out the liver, blood and bowels and otherwise detoxify the system are generally bitter and nasty tasting. Children don't like to take these herbs in liquid form (neither do adults) unless their systems really need them. As with other categories of herbs, children generally don't need the stronger tasting bitters as much as adults. They haven't had as much time to pollute their bodies as adults have. So, children can usually get by with mildly bitter herbs like alfalfa, dandelion, burdock and parsley. When they do need stronger bitters like Oregon grape, goldenseal, myrrh gum, cascara sagrada or barberry, their disagreeable taste can be partially masked by blending them with sweet tasting herbs and preparing them in a glycerine or honey base.

Finally, there is a class of herbs which are sweet tasting and/or have a slippery feel to them when moistened in the mouth. These mucilagenous herbs soothe irritations, build up weakened and depleted bodies, help tissues to heal faster, pull poisons out of the body through the bowel or skin and sometimes act as bulk-forming laxatives. These herbs are usually easy to use with children because they are not strong tasting or unpleasant. They include comfrey, slippery elm, aloe vera juice or gel, licorice root, sarsaparilla, cornsilk and marshmallow.

When you understand these basic actions of herbs, you can readily substitute one herb for another and still get good results. As you become more familiar with herbs, you will learn their subtler differences and more specific applications, but this knowledge is sufficient to get effective results with common family ailments.

PREPARING HERBS FOR CHILDREN

One of the problems people face in treating their children with herbs is finding an acceptable preparation that they will take. It isn't easy to get children to take herbs in their traditional dosage forms, especially young children. Most of the time, little children can't swallow capsules; they need a liquid dosage form. Our children generally wouldn't drink herbal teas and they dislike the taste of alcohol extracts. Besides, we don't like giving alcohol extracts to our children. Alcohol is addictive, leaves a burning sensation in the mouth and causes liver stress. It is also against our religious convictions.

Fortunately, when our oldest daughter was just one year old, we discovered a liquid form of herbs that is vastly superior to alcohol tinctures, especially for children. This is the herbal glycerite. Glycerine (or glycerol) is a natural component of all fats and oils. When fats are digested in the body, they are broken down into fatty acids and glycerine. Hence, glycerine is a non-toxic, natural food substance. It is also a good solvent of herbal constituents and a preservative. To top it off, glycerine is also sweet tasting but does not cause blood sugar problems.

Because glycerine is slightly sweet, it helps mask the disagreeable taste of many herbs. Other more pleasant tasting herbs are actually delicious when prepared in glycerine. So, by carefully selecting herbs for both taste and efficacy, it is possible to make herbal preparations which not only work, but taste great. That way, you don't have to fight your children to have them take them.

You can make a simple, herbal glycerite by simmering herbs in a mixture of 60% glycerine and 40% purified water for two to three hours. We have generally used about 1/4 cup of cut and sifted, dried herbs per 1 cup of glycerine/water solution. When you strain this solution, bottle it and store it in a cool, dark place. It retains its effectiveness for two to three years.

TincTracts™

After making simple glycerites for a couple of years, we discovered another method of making glycerites. A close friend, L. Carl Robinson, came up with a two-step method for processing herbs which he called the TincTract™ method. TincTract™ is short for TINCture/exTRACTion. I suggested adding a third step, which improved the process even further.

We were extremely pleased when we started using TincTracts™ because they tasted, smelled and worked very much like the original fresh herb. For example, the TincTract™ of alfalfa has the smell and taste of fresh mown hay. Licorice TincTract™ gives you the same taste as chewing on a stick of dried licorice root. TincTracts™ of elderberry, bayberry rootbark and sarsaparilla tasted so good that our children would ask for seconds. We found that even capsicum, lobelia and goldenseal were easier to get children to take when they were made into a TincTract™.

Unfortunately, it takes a week to make a TincTract™, so the process is impractical for home use. However, one of the three steps to making a TincTract™ makes a very suitable herbal preparation for most children's remedies. It is the step I added to the TincTract™ method. I call preparations made using this method "sealed simmer" glycerites. This preparation has some of the advantages of TincTracts™, but isn't as potent. You will find the directions for making a "sealed simmer" glycerite in the back of this book.

Some sources for obtaining commercially prepared TincTracts™, glycerites and other products suitable for children are also listed in the back of this book.

Dosages

There are two major reasons why people fail to get good results with herbs. The first is selecting the wrong type of herb and the second is failing to give a large enough dose to get the job done. Picking the wrong type of herb simply means that you picked an herb which contracts, when the problem is that the tissue is already too contracted. It is like giving soda crackers to a man dying of thirst. The crackers are not poisonous, but they don't address the problem. Learning to choose the right type of remedy merely requires some basic knowledge and experience. Fortunately, many remedies are general enough that they work for almost everything. With these general remedies, even the beginner can get good results.

The second part, giving enough dosage, is easy. Once you know the right remedy and what it is supposed to accomplish, give that remedy in small, frequently repeated doses until it works. We often give our children a dose of herbs and some water every hour until they get well. We've even given them a dose of herbs every fifteen minutes. If you don't notice any improvement after a reasonable amount of time, simply switch to another type of herb and try again.

We have a very simple method for judging how much of an herbal remedy our children need. We judge the amount to give them the same way we judge the amount of carrots, potatoes or apples they need. We give them some and then ask if they want "seconds." If they do, we give them more. If they say they've had enough, we stop. We believe in letting their bodies decide how much they require to do the job of self-healing and repair.

As mentioned earlier, we do not believe that our remedies are toxic or potentially harmful when used with any degree of prudence or common sense. When our youngest daughter was two, she climbed into the cupboard and drank half a bottle (one ounce) of one of our glycerine formulas. Did we panic and call poison control? No, we were amused. That's because we sincerely believe that these herbs are wholesome foods which the body will crave when it needs them, just like any other wholesome food. So, we give the child whatever amount it takes to help him get well—it's as simple as that.

Easy as ABC

Edward Milo Millet, a highly gifted herbalist, taught me that herb therapy was as easy as A-B-C. We can explain this by returning to the analogy of the fireplace. When the fire of life is dying we first need to fan it or *Activate* it. We also need to *Build* up the fire with proper fuel. Lastly, we need to remove the soot and ashes that may be clogging the firebox and chimney. This last step is *Cleansing*. So, all we do to heal any disease is to A-Activate (keep the body energies going), B-

Build (get good nutrition into the system) and C-Cleanse (help the body eliminate waste by making sure all four channels of elimination are working well).

This is the simple approach that has enabled us to take care of most of our family's health problems for over ten years. In the next three sections, we'll discuss each of these steps in detail and provide you with specific examples of how we've put these principles into practice in our family.

In addition, we'll devote two sections to a couple of primary concerns of parents - infection and pain. The two most commonly used types of medications are antibiotics and pain killers. We use neither in our family. So, we'll share additional information about our views on the subjects of infection and pain.

Children, like adults, also experience stress and emotional problems which contribute to illness. So, we'll briefly discuss those subjects as well.

Part Two

Activation

ctivation is supplying the body with herbal remedies and foods which give the body's energy a boost so that it will be able to complete the healing process. As an adult, I have overcome minor ailments by using activators alone. At the first sign of a cold, for example, I have taken two capsules of capsicum every hour with a large glass of water. By eating nothing else, I have been able to shake that illness off within a few hours.

As we have indicated, the body really heals itself. We don't do the healing, we merely supply raw materials and an environment which supports the body in doing its own healing. Activators are aromatic herbs which give the body the energy boost it needs to complete the job.

Children's Composition

About eight years ago, we discovered a wonderful children's remedy for activating the energy of the body for healing. We think of it as our Children's Composition formula. Composition was a formula developed by herbalist, Samuel Thomson, which he used in nearly all acute ailments. It contains 2 parts bayberry rootbark, 1 part white pine bark, 1/2 part ginger, 1/4 part cloves and 1/4 part cayenne pepper or capsicum. Thus, it has some astringent effect, to tone tissues and arrest discharges, and some aromatic effect, to stimulate healing. This formula works best when taken as a tea. I have found it beneficial for colds, flu, congestion, stomach problems, fevers and diarrhea. It is too spicy for children, though, because of the "hot" aromatics it contains.

The Children's Composition formula we discovered has essentially the same uses, but is milder and more pleasant tasting. It contains yarrow, elder flower and peppermint. While gathering wild herbs one summer, I found these three herbs and decided they would make a good fever remedy. Mixing them in equal parts I extracted them using the sealed simmer method. We were so pleased with the results, that I made a special trip to the mountains each summer to gather these herbs and make another batch.

The great herbalist, Edward Shook, says the following about the combination of elder flowers and peppermint in his *Advanced Treatise in Herbology*.

"For the treatment of colds, influenza, and fevers of all kinds, there is no remedy known to man that is so safe, sure and speedy as elder flowers, an all-around alterative, blood purifier, and general systemic cleanser. They are without a superior.

Because elder flowers are emetic and somewhat nauseating to some people, the ideal synergist to blend with them in the treatment of colds, fevers, and so forth is peppermint (*Mentha piperita*). Peppermint is a stimulant, nervine, calmative, and antiemetic, and the combination is world- famed as the greatest fever remedy ever known to man."

Considering that right after the last World War, upwards of six million people died of influenza and that millions have died since, is it not a very great privilege and blessing to be in possession of the knowledge of such a remedy? Herbalist, Henry Box of Plymouth, England says,

"For colds, influenza, fevers, inflammation of the brain, pneumonia (inflammation of the lungs), stomach, bowels or any part, this is a certain cure, I have never known it to fail, even when given up and at the point of death. It will not only save at the eleventh hour, but at the last minute of that hour. It is so harmless that you cannot use it amiss, and so effectual that you cannot give it in vain."

In the Utah mountains, yarrow blooms about the same time as the elder flowers. Yarrow was the first medicinal herb I learned to identify and use. It also has been used to help fevers and colds. The plant contains a volatile oil, similar in composition to chamomile oil, which has been medically documented to be a very effective, anti-inflammatory agent. By itself, yarrow tastes bitter, but the addition of peppermint masks this disagreeable flavor.

Most of the time, when our children are sick, we give them some of this formula. It helps promote perspiration, open the bowels, reduce inflammation, settle the stomach and calm the child. Our usual dose is about 1/4 to 1/2 teaspoonful, although I will let them have more if they want it. If the formula tastes good to them it is a sign that the body wants more. We give them the formula at least two times a day, but often we have given the child some at hourly intervals during an acute situation. We have even given this (and other formulas) as often as every 15 minutes until the illness begins to subside.

When our children have been congested I've added a little elderberry glycerite to the formula. Both elder flowers and elderberries contain substances which ease inflammation and pain. Elderberries soothe the intestines and have been used for all inflammatory bowel diseases. They have a very gentle laxative action, which may explain their decongestant properties. They also have a mild tonic action to help arrest diarrhea. Many other herbalists besides myself have observed a strong connection between bowel problems and respiratory congestion. There also appears to be a strong connection between bowel obstructions and fevers in children. So, the addition of the elderberries makes the formula even better.

Last year, I discovered that "my" favorite children's formula was an old-time pioneer remedy. A lady came into our herb shop and told me that her great-great-grandfather had been an herbalist who had helped attend to Brigham Young's family. She said that his journal records one of Brigham Young's favorite herbal formulas for treating his children. Guess what! It was composed of yarrow, elder and peppermint. Considering that Brigham Young once stated that he had not had the necessity of calling upon a doctor more than a couple of times in over twenty years, the remedy must have worked well for him.

Furthermore, while I was researching to write this book, I found an article in the June 1990 issue of *Vegetarian Times* about the elder. It gave a recipe for a fever-reducing tea: equal parts elder flowers, yarrow and peppermint. The author, Kathi Keville, calls this "a classic herbal remedy to reduce fever." She says the Iroquois Indians also used elderberries for fevers because they increased sweating and acted as a gentle laxative. And I thought I'd made a great discovery! I guess I only made a REdiscovery of a wonderful traditional remedy.

Other Activators

There are, of course, other herbs that can be used to Activate the system to aid in general healing. Straight peppermint is an excellent activator for children and one that they often will drink as a tea. You might even try making warm lemonade with peppermint in it, as this has the same basic action as Composition and my children's formula.

Another excellent activator for children is chamomile. If you recall the story of Peter Rabbit, chamomile tea was the remedy Peter Rabbit's mother gave him. Chamomile helps to settle the stomach and calm the nerves.

Catnip is another aromatic which many parents have found beneficial for their children. It also stimulates the body, settles the stomach and soothes the nerves. One famous herbal team is the combination of catnip with fennel, which has long been used as a remedy for colic, gas, and indigestion in children.

Of course, in serious cases, you may wish to go ahead and use some of the stronger aromatics such as capsicum (cayenne pepper). In fact, this is an excellent herb to have on hand in an extract form because it is one of the most powerful of all herbs for stimulating the body's energies for healing. We would never be without capsicum in our home because of its value in stopping bleeding and treating shock. Even if you do not use it internally with children, it is an excellent remedy to have on hand for external use. As we will discuss later, it is especially powerful when combined with lobelia and used as an external massage for relieving pain.

Here are some other stimulating aromatic herbs you may wish to use, should any of the above be unavailable: ginger, horseradish, cloves, cinnamon, spearmint, thyme, lemon balm, garlic and lemon grass. Many aromatic herbs make pleasant tasting teas, so you may be able to get your children to take them in that form. Experiment and try making your own children's activator formula as a sealed simmer glycerite. Maybe you can come up with an even better formula than ours.

PART THREE

Building

uilding the body isn't something you do just when your children get sick. Building the body up with good food (nutrition) is a major way to prevent disease in the first place. The biggest part of taking responsibility for the health of your own children is to take the responsibility of cultivating good health habits in your family. It isn't enough to just give your children some herbal remedies now and then. We have had to learn how to make our lifestyle healthier and use herbs for prevention as well as cure. We believe that the same thing which prevents disease will help the body cure it. So, the following information is useful whether your children are healthy or sick.

BUILDING IMMUNITY

When our oldest daughter, Sarah, was born I asked my wife to take her into the health clinic for her shots. On returning from the clinic, she told me, "I don't like that place, I don't like those people, I don't like to hear my child scream, so if you want her to have shots, then you take her because I won't." Her words brought back youthful memories of standing in line waiting for those painful shots. I remembered how I had cried and how I felt like I was being tortured and couldn't understand why. My instincts had told me that I was being violated, that something was very wrong.

Now maybe I'm just sentimental and soft, but the more I thought and prayed about it, the more I began to feel that there must be something wrong with vaccines. I believe that instinct is a gift of God and that it is a good thing, something we should pay attention to. Children are closer to their instincts than we are, therefore, their feelings about things deserve some careful consideration. I realized that my own childhood instincts told me shots were a "bad" thing. This caused me to wonder, did God intend that the only way we could protect our children against disease was through methods that caused pain and fear? I couldn't believe this was the case.

So, our family embarked on a different course. I knew that the idea of the shot was to give the person an "altered" or "weakened" case of the disease. In response, the body's immune system builds up defensive components, antibodies, which render the person "immune." In other words, the real hero is the body's immune system. The body's immune system is what protects it against the disease, not the vaccine. In fact, I have since learned that the vaccines can "backfire." That is, if the immune system is too weak or deficient to fight off the vaccine, then the body may be damaged as a result.

Since that time, I have read books which validated my reasoning. If you wish to read more on the subject, you will find some books on this topic listed in the bibliography. That way, you can read about the pro's and con's for yourself and make your own informed choice. I never tell anyone that they shouldn't vaccinate their children. That is a decision people need to make after careful thought and study, not based on my word or anybody else's. Furthermore, not everyone will be willing to do what I have been willing to do to protect my children. I decided that I was going to take the responsibility of learning how to build up my children's immune systems naturally.

My reasoning was this: if the immune system is strong and they are exposed to the disease, then the immune system will build up resistance to the disease just like it would have built up resistance to the vaccine. In fact, even if a person chooses to vaccinate their children, they still should be concerned about building up their children's immune systems, because it is the immune system fighting off the vaccine that confers immunity, not the vaccine itself.

Here are some of the things we have learned that help to build immunity:

1. Eating wholesome foods, especially fresh fruits, raw or steamed vegetables and whole grains, preferably organically grown, and avoiding sugar, white flour and other "junk" foods.

2. Providing children with daily physical and verbal expressions of love and affection such as hugs, "pats on the back" and positive feedback.

3. Providing good prenatal nutrition and care, plus nursing babies with mother's milk for at least one year (or even two if possible). In nursing, the mother transfers immune factors from her own blood into her children. This is nature's natural vaccine.

4. Giving children immune enhancing herbs and nutritional supplements.

In other words, don't expect your children to be healthy, strong and resistant to disease if you are consuming a typical American diet and subjecting your children to constant mental and emotional stress. Health is created by observing healthy habits. It is part of the law of the harvest: "As you sow, so shall you reap."

FEEDING CHILDREN

Healthy bodies require healthy food and that doesn't mean the processed, refined and "enriched" foods of modern affluent society. We buy wholesome food, even if it appears to cost more, because we know we will pay the price later in the form of sickness and doctor bills. The truth is, however, that eating healthy is actually easier on the family budget. Organically grown produce, 100% whole-grain bread and other similar foods may cost more than their refined counterparts, but, on the other hand, children will eat less and remain healthier. That's because these foods are more nutritionally dense. That is, they contain more vitamins and minerals and hence are more satisfying to the body.

If your children aren't used to eating wholesome foods, you will need to be patient as you work to "convert" them. We've had friends over to our home whose children wouldn't eat anything we served. They "turned their noses up" at our vegetables and whole grains. All these children wanted was junk food. If your children are like this, you may need to give them a lesson in nutrition before you try to make changes in their diet. If they have been sick, you might explain to them that eating too much "junk food" could be the reason why they are sick. Tell them that their bodies will be healthier and stronger if they eat more wholesome foods.

When changing children's diets, focus on the positive. Place vegetables like carrot and celery sticks out for them to eat as you are preparing the meal. If they are hungry enough they will eat this wholesome food first while waiting for something else. Gradually substitute raw honey, pure maple syrup and other natural sweeteners for refined sugar. Children love sweets, so make wholesome sweets for them. Increase portions of vegetables, fruits, nuts, seeds and whole grains while decreasing portions of meat and dairy foods.

Don't try to control everything your children eat. That tends to engender rebellion. A little "treat" now and then shouldn't hurt them if their general diet is good. Instead, teach them in a positive manner the benefits of eating wholesome foods. They need to learn to control themselves. You can't watch them constantly. If one of my children has a piece of candy he got from a friend, I let him eat it and enjoy it. I just don't buy it for him. If he offers me a piece, I simply say, "I don't eat that, it doesn't make me feel good." I hope he will learn by my example, not my preaching.

There are many good books on nutrition and healthy cooking. Check the bibliography in the back of this book and your local health food store for others.

THYMUS THERAPY

Likewise, we have found that immunity is directly connected to self-esteem. The thymus gland, which regulates the immune system, is right under the breastbone. It is the spot we point to when we say "me." Part of immunity is the ability to distinguish what is self from what is not self. In other words, our bodies have to be able to recognize who the enemy is. That sense of who and what I AM is part of our ability to stand up and defend ourselves on every level, including fighting disease.

There is ample research to demonstrate that when we are depressed, tired, worried, fearful, anxious, sad, etc., that our immune system's function diminishes. Likewise, when we are happy, positive, loving and hopeful, our immunity increases. This is true in both adults and children. That is why both adults and children tend to get sick when they are under STRESS.

So, if we run our children down with constant criticism, threats, fighting and quarreling, we shouldn't be surprised if they become sickly. Likewise, we all know that we feel better when we are sick if someone shows us a little love and tender care. Love, then, is one of the greatest healers and builders of the immune system that we know. We need to "vaccinate" our children with it several times every day so they can stand up to the stresses of the world.

We do this through hugs, pats on the back and kind words. It is interesting that when we hug, we hold people to our breast. We press our thymus area to their thymus area. We call this a "thymus to thymus" hug or a "thymus treatment." When we pat someone on the back, we pat them in the area of the thymus. Hence, a pat on the back, physically or verbally, is a stimulation to the self-esteem and hence to the immune-regulating power of the thymus gland. Kind words of encouragement that help children feel good about themselves will also go a long way in building their resistance to disease.

Herbal "Vaccines"

Now, let's talk about herbs which can build a child's resistance to disease. One of the best herbs for the immune system is *Echinacea angustifolia*. This plant has been dubbed by researchers as a non-specific immuno-stimulant. This plant contains a substance which inhibits the spread of bacterial infection. It appears to activate and stimulate the production of white blood cells. According to Daniel B. Mowrey in *Next Generation Herbal Medicine*, the plant was used by the American eclectic physicians to both prevent and treat a wide variety of bacterial and viral infections, such as: smallpox, typhoid, tetanus, diphtheria, syphilis, influenza, tuberculosis, yellow fever, malaria, polio, measles, rubella, whooping cough, mumps, cholera and the common cold. The plant also has no known toxicity.

Given the impressive research and history behind this herb, I decided to make an immune formula for my children with this herb as the principle ingredient. I combined *Echinacea angustifolia* with Missouri snakeroot (*Parthenium integrifolium*) and thyme. Missouri snakeroot has also been used as an immuno-stimulant. Thyme is thought to stimulate the thymus gland, which regulates the immune system. It is also a powerful antiseptic and disinfectant and has been used to break up mucus, fight colds, coughs, fevers, headaches and sore throats.

We give this formula to our children as a preventative to keep them healthy, especially through the winter months. The usual dose is about 1/2 teaspoonful before bed or first thing in the morning, but we might give more if there is something "going around." We also give our children this formula when they are sick, usually about every two hours, combined with the Children's Composition formula. This is because the immune-boosting effect of echinacea lasts about two hours. It may also be used internally and externally when a child is injured, as echinacea helps to prevent and contain infection in wounds.

We've produced several versions of this formula. In my most recent version, I have dropped the Missouri snakeroot and added licorice and elderberries. This not only improves the taste, but these herbs also enhance the effect. We've discussed the properties of elderberries, but we should add some information here about licorice root.

Licorice is a wonderful herb for children. The Chinese use it as a catalyst in many of their formulas. It stimulates and builds the adrenal glands, which help the body cope with stress. It also stabilizes blood sugar levels. Like adults, children get cranky, irritable and even depressed when their blood sugar levels drop. The adrenals are the home of the body's "fight." Strong adrenals mean that children will have more power to face the challenges of life, both emotional and physical.

Licorice contains glycyrrhizin, a substance which is many times sweeter than sugar. Because of its natural sweetness, licorice is very helpful in masking the taste of many bitter herbs in a liquid formula without destroying their therapeutic effects. Therefore, it is a useful addition to many children's formulas.

Other immune-building herbs you may want to consider for your children include: goldenseal, Oregon grape, garlic, pau d'arco, chaparral, red clover, myrrh gum, barberry rootbark and astragalus. However, many of these are very nasty tasting and will need to be skillfully combined with more pleasant tasting herbs in a glycerine base in order to get your children to enjoy taking them.

HERBAL MINERALS

One of the greatest problems with nutrition today is the lack of trace minerals in our food. Even if we are feeding our children right, today's commercially grown food does not have the trace mineral value of foods grown 50 or 100 years ago. These trace minerals are depleted by our agricultural practices as well as by refining. We are not talking about major minerals like calcium, magnesium and phosphorus, but elements that are needed only in very tiny quantities, like chromium, boron, manganese, silicon and zinc. Many of these minerals are very important for growth and development of body tissues, catalyzing hormones and for building immunity.

We feel that the best way to get minerals is in whole plant foods, not in artificial mineral supplements. We also feel that the TincTract™ process helps extract these trace minerals better than any other herb process we've seen to date. We taught the TincTract™ process to our midwife, Joan Patton, who has used it for many years to make a formula she calls Liquid Calcium. We call it Herbal Minerals, because the herbs in it contain many other elements besides calcium. This formula contains several mineral-rich herbs, including: alfalfa, borage, chickweed, oatstraw, horsetail (shavegrass) and red raspberry. These herbs contain elements like silicon and manganese, as well as calcium. The formula also contains several activating herbs: yarrow, peppermint, chamomile and dill, which aid digestion and assimilation.

Joan finds giving Herbal Minerals to pregnant mothers eliminates many complications during pregnancy and delivery. It has also helped produce healthier babies. Many women become trace mineral deficient during pregnancy because the baby is getting first choice of the elements in her body. These trace mineral deficiencies can produce symptoms like mood swings, hair loss, connective tissue weakness, bone weakness and even morning sickness.

My wife has used Herbal Minerals during two pregnancies and it has helped tremendously with keeping iron and calcium levels up in her body. We have been completely sold on the formula. However, we've also extended its use to many other problems as well.

One of our sons was seven years old and had still not lost any of his baby teeth. The dentist informed us that his adult teeth appeared to be forming naturally, but were not descending. We started giving him 1/2 teaspoon of the Herbal Minerals TincTract™ each day and within just six weeks he had lost six baby teeth and had four adult teeth come in. We have since used Herbal Minerals to help with other structural or developmental problems with good success.

We also found that giving 1/2 teaspoon of Herbal Minerals along with 1/2 teaspoon of licorice root TincTract™ just prior to bedtime solved a bedwetting problem with both of our sons. Many people have tried all sorts of kidney herbs for this problem with no success, but when we heard Dr. Lendon Smith, M.D. at a lecture say that bedwetting can be a blood sugar problem with a mineral imbalance we decided to try this approach. It worked well for us and has since worked well for others.

We've also seen Herbal Minerals help build resistance to disease, speed healing of injuries and some people have told us that it helps with hyperactivity and sleep disorders. We do not know all the possibilities for this formula, but we do need to stress that we don't believe that the formula is actually solving these problems. The formula is simply a nutritional supplement and is providing the body with certain essential elements in an easily assimilated form. The body is doing the healing, just as it always does whenever it has the raw materials it needs.

You could try making sealed simmer glycerites out of some mineral-rich herbs for your own children. However, the sealed simmer glycerite is not as potent as a TincTract™, so you would probably need to administer larger amounts.

Older children can take mineral-rich herbs in capsule form. An excellent combination is kelp, alfalfa and dandelion. Other mineral-rich herbs you might give your children include: horsetail, oatstraw, parsley, dulse, Irish moss and red raspberry.

NATURAL RESISTANCE

Does our approach to building the strength and immunity of our children work? We think so. Our children are very resistant to disease and they appear to become more resistant to disease as time goes on. When they do get sick, they usually recover remarkably fast. Their symptoms are less severe, too.

For example, when our oldest daughter got the chicken pox, she never really acted sick. She was never feverish or lethargic. In fact, she complained when we wouldn't let her go out and play with the other children because she was covered with pox. My wife believes that chicken pox ought to be gotten over with when you're a child, because it can be a serious illness if you catch it as an adult. So she has deliberately exposed the three younger children to other children with chicken pox in hopes they would catch it. When she had exposed Ezra Arthur, our third child, to chicken pox twice, he failed to catch it. Then, one day she called some friends of ours to find out if our children could go play with theirs. The mom said no because her children had chicken pox. My wife said, "Oh, that's great, please let my children go play with your children so they will catch it." I'm sure that the other mom thought my wife was a little strange, especially since her husband is a medical doctor, but she agreed. I happened to be upset because I was very busy at the time and said, "I don't want to have to take care of sick children." My wife replied, "If they get sick, I'll take care of them."

Well, a couple of weeks later I was playing with my younger daughter and I noticed she had a funny red mark on her forehead. I said, "What happened? Did she get bit by a mosquito or something?" "No," my wife said, "she has chicken pox." "Chicken pox?" "Yes," she said, "she's had them for two days. Ezra has them, too." Since neither of these children had acted sick at all, and most of the pox were hidden by their clothes, I hadn't even noticed. Needless to say, they recovered very quickly with a few simple herbal remedies.

RESTORING THE FLAME

Eating tends to interfere with the healing process. Hippocrates' famous saying, "Feed a cold, starve a fever" actually means "If you feed a cold, you'll HAVE to starve a fever." Fasting is one way to help the body clean out the debris that it is trying to eliminate. In fact, most children and animals have the instinctive desire to refrain from food and even drink when they are sick.

This is because it does no good to throw logs on a dying fire. When our body's inner "fire" is smoldering and the eliminative organs are blocked, throwing heavy food into the system merely causes more congestion. Hence, if our children aren't hungry when they are sick, we don't force them to eat. Instead, we need to give them some simple herbs to A-Activate their systems and keep their energy up and then go to C-Cleansing herbs to help remove the obstructions from their system. If they are hungry, we only let them eat soups, broths, juices or other simple foods that will not further "clog" their systems.

When we build the body system back from a state of sickness to health, we follow the same procedure you would use in refueling a dying fire. You start with fine kindling and small sticks and gradually build up the heat until you can again throw on heavy logs. Raw fruit and vegetable juices or soups (like grandma's famous chicken soup) can be likened to the fine kindling we use to help re-ignite the flame of life. As the child starts to feel better we gradually introduce vegetables, nuts, seeds and proteins back into his diet, just like you would start adding bigger and bigger sticks to the fire.

Our family are not vegetarians, nor are we rabid fanatics about avoiding all junk food. We feel a little "treat" now and then is not seriously damaging when the general diet is a good one. However, we do have special rules which go into effect when someone is sick. When our children are sick or congested, they can't have any heavy protein foods such as meat, fish, chicken, eggs, milk, cheese or even tofu. They also can't have any refined foods. Their diet is limited to fruits, vegetables and a modest amount of whole grains, nuts, seeds and legumes until their bodies recover.

PART FOUR

Cleansing

leansing is a critical step in natural healing. It was over ten years ago we first learned the concept that disease symptoms are the body's attempt to clear obstructions clogging the system. Our experiences since that time have convinced us that the best way to treat most minor ailments is to open the four channels of elimination to help the body get rid of what is bothering it. These four channels are the bowels, the kidneys, the skin and the respiratory tract.

Anyone of these channels can be a vehicle through which the body tries to eliminate material that is the real cause of disease. If the body eliminates through the bowel, the result will be nausea, vomiting and diarrhea. When it tries to eliminate through the skin, it will produce rashes, pimples, hives, acne, dandruff, itching and body odor. When it tries to eliminate through the respiratory tract, it can cause runny noses, watery eyes, sneezing, post-nasal drip, earaches, sore throats, tonsillitis, bronchitis, bad breath, coughs and congestion in the lungs. When the problem lies with the kidneys it can cause frequent urination, burning urination, back pain and leg cramps.

Rather than trying to suppress these symptoms, our goal should be to make them more productive; that is, to help the body do what it is trying to do, i.e., to eliminate whatever is clogging it. So, let's look at some herbs and procedures which can help the body in its efforts to remove this waste.

The Bowel

In spite of what some doctors might say to the contrary, our experience has convinced us that our grandmothers and great-grandmothers were right when they stressed the importance of staying regular with the bowels.

We have never had an occasion when one of our children was feverish, where they were not feeling well again 30 minutes after the obstructions had been removed from the bowel. Likewise, we have seen much improvement in coughs, runny noses, flu, headaches, diarrhea, sore throats and even earaches when the bowel is cleansed.

ENEMAS

The fastest way to open the "chimney" of the bowel is with an enema. This is a simple procedure and properly done, is both safe and effective. I have been surprised at the number of parents who are afraid to give their children an enema, but it is not that difficult. To give an enema to a child you will need a bulb syringe, some petroleum jelly or similar lubricant and an enema solution.

My favorite enema solution is garlic "tea." Garlic is a wonderful natural antibiotic. It is as powerful as penicillin without the side-effects. In my experience, I have found it to be superior to antibiotics in fighting many common ailments. I have made my enema solution one of three ways: (1) By blending a small clove of fresh garlic with a pint of warm water in the blender and then straining to remove the pulp. (I quit doing this because my wife didn't like the odor it left in the blender). (2) You can also make garlic tea by steeping two or three capsules of garlic powder (about a quarter of a teaspoonful) in a cup of boiling water. Be sure to strain it through a fine cloth to remove the fiber particles. (3) I have found the simplest method is to put a couple of dropperfuls of garlic oil (oil which has been diluted in olive oil) into a teacup full of warm water. Stir the solution. Although the oil will float to the top, enough garlic will permeate the water to be effective.

Another favorite enema solution is catnip tea. Use three or four capsules of catnip powder or about 1 teaspoon of cut and sifted catnip herb per cup of boiling water. Other similar herbs could also be used such as peppermint or chamomile. The Children's Composition formula also makes an "instant" enema solution. Simply add 1 teaspoon of the glycerite to a cup of warm water.

Always test the enema solution to make sure it is warm, not hot or cold. If you place a couple of drops on your wrist, it should feel neutral in temperature (like testing a baby bottle).

Lie the child on his left side and lubricate the anal opening. Also lubricate the tip of the syringe. Explain to the child that this will feel uncomfortable, but that it will help him feel better. Be gentle, but firm about it. If you were taking the child to the doctor, the child might get a shot which would hurt worse and you'd probably make them hold still for that. An enema is no where near as uncomfortable as a shot, so have him hold still. I always talk to my children in a loving, but firm manner. Fill the syringe with the enema solution by squeezing the syringe and then sucking up the solution. Turn the syringe upright and squeeze any remaining air out of it. Now you can fill it completely full.

Gently insert the tip of the syringe into the anus. Then give a gentle squeeze. If you encounter strong resistance, or the child seems to be in pain, stop squeezing and withdraw the syringe. Make sure you don't "suck" with the syringe as you withdraw.

With a baby, however, put a diaper on the baby's bottom and then wrap his bottom in a towel. (Enemas can make the stool "runny" and you don't want it to leak onto you.) Then cuddle and hold the baby for a few minutes.

If nothing comes out, repeat the process again. It may take several tries before anything passes, but don't be concerned. Putting in a small amount of fluid every five minutes will not hurt the bowel. In fact, often small children get dehydrated when they are feverish because they do not drink enough fluids, so the body will absorb all of the liquid put into the bowel. This seems to actually be beneficial.

With an older child, tell them they can go "potty" if they need to. If they don't, then repeat the process. Wait a minute or two and put a little more fluid in.

The stool should be soft. If only a small amount of hard stool is passed, you may need to repeat the process again, until a soft stool passes. The trick is to get the bowel to move freely.

CHILDHOOD AILMENTS

Let us share with you a few stories of how enemas have helped our family.

With the support and encouragement of our midwife, we even gave an enema to a one-day old baby. Our third child, Ezra Arthur, was very fussy or colicky during the first 24 hours after his birth. Our midwife told us that he had probably swallowed some fluid during birth and the material in his bowels was irritating his body. After giving him an enema with a little garlic tea, he passed some blackish-green stringy material and immediately afterward fell into a peaceful slumber.

One night, when he was about 18 months old, Ezra Arthur woke us up in the middle of the night. He was burning hot with a fever. (I don't know how many degrees because we never bother to take the child's temperature if he has a fever, we just commence treatment immediately until the fever comes down. We have always been able to eliminate the fever in a few hours at the most.) I prepared a solution of garlic oil and water and gave him a syringe full. He didn't pass anything, but he started to perspire, "cooled down" and fell asleep.

That, by-the-way, is another benefit of the herbal solutions. Garlic, peppermint, catnip, yarrow, chamomile and other aromatic herbs all help to promote perspiration, which also helps the body to evacuate poisons and lower the body temperature. So, rather than wake him up, we just let him sleep.

About two hours later, however, Ezra awakened with a burning fever. I gave him, rectally, more garlic solution; again he perspired, cooled down and fell asleep. In the morning, he was feverish again. I gave him another round of the enema solution, but this time, I also sat in the rocking chair and gently rubbed his belly (not massaged, just lightly rubbed). I thought that there might be an obstruction that needed help. After about 15 minutes, Ezra strained very hard and when I checked his diaper, I found that he had passed a small ball of peanut pieces.

Apparently, the night before he had gotten into a jar of peanuts while he was with a baby-sitter and having only front teeth and no molars, he had only been able to crack and swallow them in large pieces. They had lodged in the bowel and the body had created a fever to try and expel the obstruction. Anyway, a half hour later, you never would have known that the child had ever been sick. He was running around like a normal toddler should, happy and bright.

A few times medically oriented people have challenged me on these experiences. One such person said, "How did you know your child was really well? Did you have a doctor make the diagnosis that the child was sick and verify the child was well? How did you know there wasn't a serious infection present which you were ignoring?" To me, such questions border on paranoia. Good grief! Do we have to have an expert tell us everything? Have we no common sense left in our society? A sick child acts sick! Any parent can tell the difference between when their child is sick and when their child is well, and probably better than most doctors could because they live with the child.

A sick child is lethargic, tired, hot, congested, constipated or in pain. Parental instinct can often pick up the fact that something is wrong before it becomes serious. A healthy child runs, jumps, plays, laughs and gets into everything. So, when I say that I have seen fevers completely gone within a half hour after the bowel was cleared, I'm saying the child was WELL. They no longer felt or acted sick for the rest of the day or the days that followed.

CHILDREN'S LAXATIVES

Enemas are not the only way to get a child's bowels moving. One night one of our children seemed a little warm and just bordering on getting sick. So we gave him a couple of squirts of blue vervain in glycerine before bedtime. The next morning the child had a very messy bowel movement (I know, I changed the diaper) and was completely well. We have had similar experiences on other occasions.

Children rarely need harsh herbal laxatives like cascara sagrada or senna. Usually, all they need is a little raw apple juice, some ripe cherries or that good old stand-by, prune juice. We can stave off a lot of problems by making sure our children have plenty of fiber-rich fresh fruits, raw vegetables and whole grains instead of white bread, meat and dairy products.

Herbs like licorice root, elderberries, flaxseed, slippery elm and blue vervain may also be helpful in getting children's bowels to move. Actually, glycerine has a mild laxative action as well, an added benefit of using herbal glycerites to treat common ailments.

If children do need a stronger laxative, give them a glycerite of cascara sagrada combined with some nervines like chamomile and peppermint. The nervines will help prevent cascara's tendency to cause cramping or "griping." You will also want to try to disguise the bitter taste of cascara with some licorice, fennel, anise and/or elderberries. These herbs will also mellow out the laxative formula so its action won't be too harsh. There is a commercial herb formula called Kid's Cascara Blend which was designed in this manner.

Digestive Problems

Many bowel problems begin with poor digestion. Colicky babies often have digestive weakness, for example. Headaches may be caused by a sour stomach, too. So, let's consider briefly a few remedies for indigestion, flu and upset stomachs. One of the traditional remedies for children's digestive problems is catnip & fennel. I have combined meadowsweet with this traditional duo to make a formula I call Super Catnip & Fennel. This combination of herbs is excellent for colic, upset stomachs, gas, nausea, diarrhea, food allergies and other bowel problems. It can be made into a tea or used as an herbal glycerite.

Another wonderful remedy for digestive problems is papaya fruit and peppermint. This can be taken in tea, powder or tablet form. It is sweet, delicious and children won't mind this remedy at all. There are also papaya enzyme tablets which are tasty and beneficial.

Other herbs which may be helpful for digestive problems in children include: peppermint, catnip, ginger, chamomile and safflowers. I have used both my Children's Composition formula (yarrow, elder flowers and peppermint) and my children's nervine formula (chamomile, peppermint, hops and passion flower) to settle upset stomachs. Because these herbs all help to settle the stomach, they are very beneficial in cases of the flu.

While we are on the subject, let me mention one other remedy we would never be without - activated charcoal. Activated charcoal absorbs gases and poisons that upset the digestive tract, making it an excellent remedy for diarrhea, food poisoning, nausea, foul belching and sour stomachs in both children and adults. Because charcoal adsorbs most poisons, it is a remedy that we always try to have around in case of accidental poisoning. Should one of our children accidently ingest a poison, the first remedy I would reach for is charcoal. It can be administered by diluting it in a little water and getting the child to take it from a spoon or in a dropper. It isn't exactly tasty, but it works very well. Of course, we would also call the local poison control center for further instructions. Nevertheless, charcoal is worth having in your first aid kit for emergencies.

By the way, charcoal can also be applied to insect bites, bee stings and even spider bites as a poultice to help draw the poisons out of the skin. Simply moisten the charcoal with a little water and apply it as a paste. For more information on the uses of activated charcoal pick up a copy of the book *Rx Charcoal* by Agatha and Calvin Thrash.

Another item which is milder, but helpful for similar problems, is slippery elm. This mucilaginous herb also helps absorb toxins in the bowel. In fact, it is very soothing to the entire digestive system. It is useful especially for diarrhea, bowel weakness or as a mild nourishing food for sick children. Since the herb is slightly sweet, it is one that children will often take readily if it is mixed in some cereal, apple sauce or fruit juice. We have also blended it with fruit juice and used it to make a "mock" chocolate drink by mixing it with hot milk and honey.

The Skin

The skin is the body's largest eliminative organ. Through the sweat and oil glands in the skin, the body can eliminate waste material from the blood and lymph more rapidly than by any other means. Hence, opening this eliminative channel is vital to cleaning out the body.

SWEAT BATHS

At the first sign of a cold, I usually take an enema and a sweat bath. These two procedures insure that these major channels of elimination are open and working. We've already discussed enemas; here we will introduce you to the sweat bath.

Traditionally, sweat baths have been taken in sweat lodges or saunas. American pioneers would wrap a person sitting in a chair in blankets and place a hot stone in a pail at his feet. By pouring water into the pail, the steam would come up under the blankets until he started to perspire.

With modern, hot running water and bathtubs, it isn't necessary to go to this much trouble. We simply sit in a tub of water as hot as we can tolerate. To the water we add a couple of tablespoons of ginger powder, a handful of rosemary or mint leaves or other aromatic herbs. It is best to put the herbs into a little cloth bag (like a large tea bag) so you don't have to clean them out of the tub. Another alternative is to add a quarter teaspoon of lavender oil, tea tree oil, or some other pure essential oil. These herbs encourage blood flow to the extremities and stimulate the sweat glands. Drink plenty of water before sitting in the bath or better yet, a fragrant herbal tea.

After you get out of the bath, wrap yourself in a cotton sheet and go to bed. Pile on the blankets and allow yourself to sweat freely. You may even fall asleep. When you arise, take a cool shower to cleanse the skin and close your pores. Don't allow yourself to take a chill.

With small children, you don't want to put them into a really hot bath, so we use a warm bath and gently wash their body down with some natural soap and a wash cloth to make certain their pores are open. Adding just a small amount of lavender oil or tea tree oil to the bath, or using Dr. Bonner's Peppermint soap will help to stimulate the circulation and draw the blood to the extremities.

We have found sweat baths to be helpful for all types of acute ailments, including colds, fevers, earaches and so forth. Lavender oil seems to be a very nice addition to the bath for children as it is very calming and relaxing.

DRAWING BATHS

Sometimes it is necessary to help draw poisons out through the skin by means of an herbal bath or external application. We have found a bath with Redmond clay, Epsom salts or comfrey tea can be very beneficial for children with itching, chicken pox, measles or hives. We have also heard good reports about using Herbal Trim skin conditioner for this purpose.

When our children have had measles or chicken pox, we have used blood purifiers both internally and externally. We have given them in enemas and orally. When our oldest daughter had the chicken pox, we gave her an enema and applied a solution of goldenseal and yellow dock to her skin. She was hardly sick at all and her poxes healed up in just a couple of days without any problem.

Blood Purifiers

Whenever there are skin eruptions of any kind, including acne, pimples, rashes and pox, herbalists have treated these conditions with herbs known as blood purifiers. Blood purifiers are herbs which strengthen the blood-building organs such as the liver and the spleen. These are the kind of herbs grandmothers used to give their children as "tonics." Herbalists believe that skin eruptions are the body's way of removing impurities from the blood. Blood purifiers help to accelerate this process so that the body is able to finish this eliminative process more quickly and with less discomfort.

My favorite blood purifier for children is sarsaparilla. We have used sarsaparilla as a single herb in TincTract™ form and in combination with other herbs to "clean" the blood. Sarsaparilla was one of the herbs used to flavor old-fashioned root beer, so we have called the sarsaparilla liquid our "root beer extract." I've often given it to my children as a reward for taking something less pleasant such as goldenseal.

My recipe for a children's blood purifier includes sarsaparilla and two other completely non-toxic blood purifiers: dandelion and burdock. Both dandelion and burdock have been eaten as vegetables by various peoples throughout the world. So, they are completely safe for children. I also add chamomile to this formula as my activator herb. We'll talk more about chamomile later.

Our midwife, Joan, uses the TincTract™ of safflowers as a blood purifer, too. Safflowers help to improve the digestive power of the stomach. Many herbalists feel they are a natural supplement to improve hydrochloric acid in the stomach. We've also had good results with relieving sore muscles with safflowers and lots of water. Safflowers help to neutralize lactic acid build-up in the muscles. Joan recommends safflowers for eruptive diseases like measles and chicken pox. She also recommended it for mild jaundice in our youngest baby.

Other blood purifying herbs you might consider include: Oregon grape, red clover, alfalfa, yucca, yellow dock and red beets. Here again, you can experiment with different combinations to determine what tastes and works the best.

Measles, Pox and Acne

We mentioned our children's natural resistance to disease by telling about our experiences with chicken pox. We've used a number of things to help external itching and aid healing pox and measles. With our oldest daughter we applied a mixture of goldenseal and yellow dock to relieve itching and help the pox to heal. When our youngest daughter had chicken pox, a couple were in her private area that itched and made her uncomfortable. The itching is due to the poisons that are trying to be eliminated through the skin. So, I gave her some Oregon grape and blue vervain in glycerine to take internally. Then I sat her in a warm bath and rubbed Oregon grape liquid herb all over the top of her body. I let it just soak in through the skin. Two such treatments completely eliminated the itching and helped the pox to heal very quickly.

We have friends who have had excellent results in relieving itching with a comfrey tea bath. Another herbalist has found that a mixture of aloe vera and other herbs sold commercially as Herbal Trim has been very beneficial for itching, bites and other skin problems. It was formulated to draw poisons out of the fat layer under the skin. Itching is caused by poisons accumulating in this area which are unable to get out of the body. Once you draw them out of the body, the itching stops.

Acne is another common skin eruption which can be treated with blood purifers. Usually you will want to use the stronger blood purifiers like chaparral, red clover and yellow dock. Using these liver-strengthening herbs may also help mood swings, blood sugar imbalances, hormonal problems, food allergies and headaches which teenagers often have. Externally, Redmond clay may be applied to draw the poisons out of the body and help the body get rid of the pimple.

The Respiratory Passages

SINUSES

Many parents get worried about the slightest sniffle in their children. Commonly, parents run their children to the doctor for colds, coughs and other respiratory ailments for antibiotics. However, antibiotics kill bacteria and since colds are believed to be a viral condition, antibiotics don't help colds at all. Many other people use antihistamines. These drugs dry up the sinuses and provide temporary relief. But in the long run, they can make sinus problems worse.

Excessive drainage is caused by inflammation of the sinus membranes due to the presence of some irritating substance. When the tissues are damaged by irritants they release histamines which dilate the blood capillaries and allow excess fluid to enter the tissue spaces.

Under normal conditions, the lymphatic system picks up excess fluid and irritating substances and cleans them up in the lymph nodes. Under certain conditions, however, the lymphatic system can be overburdened and the excess fluid and waste seeps out of the mucus membranes instead.

If this continues for long periods, it can weaken the tissues in that area, causing more severe problems. Also, if we buy the idea that germs feed on waste, then an ideal breeding ground for germs is set up, which could lead to sinus infections or other more serious problems.

Most natural healers have concluded that excessive consumption of dairy products, and in some cases other heavy protein foods, put too a great a burden on the lymphatic system, congesting it and making a person more prone to sinus problems. We have also observed that sugar and salt tend to aggravate these conditions. Our children tend to get sick during the holidays when well-meaning teachers, friends and family (including their parents) give them too many "treats." Hence, when our children are congested, the first rule is NO dairy (especially milk), salt, sugar or meat.

Where the problems are chronic, we find that the digestive system may be weak and proteins are only partially digested. Undigested proteins can cause allergic reactions. Hence, children may need a digestive aid such as a papaya mint tablet, or some activating herbs like chamomile, peppermint or safflowers for their digestive systems. Children with sinus troubles usually have bowel problems as well and need to get their bowels moving properly.

The secret of getting rid of respiratory congestion is to use small, frequently repeated doses of herbs which help clear the lymph channels and the bowel. We most frequently use our Children's Composition formula for this purpose, but we have also developed a stronger formula for more persistent problems. This formula contains: red root, echinacea purpurea, yarrow flowers, myrrh gum, red clover tops and Oregon grape root.

Lymphatic Congestion

Red root is an herb we found that helps to shrink swollen lymph nodes, raise the platelet count and shrink a swollen spleen. In this formula I combined it with another species of echinacea, which also helps to cleanse and rebuild the lymph system used with other infection fighters and blood purifiers. We have had good results with this formula with chronic respiratory congestion, swollen lymph nodes, tonsillitis, frequent ear infections and the like.

Generally, we use it in conjunction with an aromatherapy blend which we rub into the swollen lymph nodes. The volatile oils penetrate right through the skin into the blood and lymph where they strengthen the body's ability to fight infection and clean out the debris. To make this oil we mix cajuput or tea tree oil with lemon oil, lavender oil, clove oil and myrrh oil in a base of olive oil. Here again, a variety of articles could probably be used, but this is the formula we have had the best results with. We have rubbed it into the throat for sore throats, swollen lymph nodes, tonsillitis, laryngitis and the like with good results. We have also used a few drops in the ear for earaches and a drop or two directly to the back of the throat for sore throats.

Lungs

If your child ever has a deep cough, put your ear against his back or chest and listen to his lungs. Chances are you'll hear a rumbling, grave sound that will make you feel very uncomfortable. Years ago, a chiropractor friend told me that you could help clear the lungs by massaging warm olive oil into the back and chest. You start at the backbone and massage the oil in between the ribs and then around to the sides. Massage the lymph nodes under the armpits and continue the massage around to the breastbone. Particularly massage in between the ribs above the breast area.

It works, but I found it works much better if you use some essential oils in the olive oil. Garlic oil works great, but I found that I needed to dilute it with more olive oil because it was much too strong straight. If the child's sinuses are plugged up, he won't mind the garlic oil because he can't smell it. However, you might find it difficult to rock him to sleep after this application.

I also tried combining a commercial blend of essential oils, Tei Fu, with the olive oil. However, I found the best (and most pleasant results) when I made my own blend of essential oils. Oils like eucalyptus, wintergreen, camphor, menthol and others have a long history of use for opening respiratory passages. There are over-the-counter cold preparations which contain these ingredients. Other oils you may wish to add (in smaller amounts) include: thyme oil, lavender oil, cajuput oil or tea tree oil. Dilute these essential oils with at least five parts of olive oil or some other fixed oil before applying them externally so as not to irritate the skin.

I have repeatedly seen one application of this oil, used as described above, clear up the lungs in less than 24 hours. Of course, I usually couple this with my usual dosage of our Children's Composition formula and an herbal cough syrup.

Coughs

The lungs constantly secrete a thin coating of mucus to lubricate and protect these delicate membranes. Tiny hair-like projections called cilia sweep this mucus up to the throat where it is swallowed when we "clear our throat". The mucus traps particles of dust, smoke, or pollen, which are present in the air we breathe. Then the cilia sweep the mucus and debris out of the lungs. Sometimes, however, the mucus may become "stuck." This may be due to a drying out of the mucus membranes, an infection, or in the herbalist's point of view, because the body is trying to eliminate toxic debris through the mucus. When this happens, the body creates a reflex action called a cough which tries to break up the stuck mucus and expel it from the lungs.

In other words, the cough is not the problem; it is the body's attempt to solve the problem. Over-the-counter cough preparations all contain cough suppressants, substances which deaden the nervous reflex and stop the coughing. This may help the child to sleep, but it does not help to remove the underlying cause of the problem. Traditionally, herbalists have used expectorants to treat coughs. An expectorant is an agent which helps to promote a healthy flow of mucus onto the mucus membranes to break up the congested mucus and help the body expel it. In other words, an expectorant makes the cough productive. It helps the cough reflex work to get rid of the problem.

My favorite expectorant is a combination of white pine bark, wild cherry bark and spikenard. It tastes so good I call it Wonderful Wild Cherry. All of these herbs are old-time remedies for coughs and at one time were used in over-the-counter cough preparations. I have also toyed with adding elderberries, cinnamon, licorice, lobelia and honey. Mixed up right, these herbs taste good enough to use as a pancake syrup, and that's no exaggeration.

There are many other expectorants you might try. We've had good results with raw honey and fresh lemon juice, for example. We've also purchased some over-the-counter preparations like Olbas Cough Syrup and Ricola Natural Cough Drops. Our children like both of these products. The glycerite of yerba santa is especially useful for deep coughs and congestion (although it isn't particularly tasty). Other expectorant herbs include: balm of Gilead, horehound, elecampane, lobelia, garlic and eucalyptus.

Asthma

Although we have never had an asthmatic child, we know of many people who have worked with asthmatic children. The same basic rules and procedures apply here as apply with other respiratory problems. Here are the things we would do if we had an asthmatic child:

First, we would clean up his diet. We would take him off ALL dairy products, refined sugars and processed flours. We would also limit his protein intake. We would feed him lots of fresh fruits, vegetables and whole grains. We would probably also give him a mineral supplement such as the Herbal Minerals or a colloidial mineral supplement (Aromin) to build up his mineral reserves.

Secondly, we would give him the herbs that help to clear up the respiratory congestion as described above. This includes cleaning out his bowel as well as giving him aids to clear the respiratory congestion.

Thirdly, asthma appears to be stress related. In fact, when the doctor treats an asthmatic child, he often gives him a shot of the adrenal hormone ephinephrine. Licorice root helps build the adrenals and aids the body's ability to cope with stress. So we would probably give our child licorice root and/or other adaptagenic herbs such as ginseng, suma, schizandra or astragalus. We would also give the child nervine herbs, such as the formula described under emotional remedies. We might even try some flower essences.

Fourthly, many children with asthma have digestive problems. They are having difficulty digesting proteins, meat, dairy products and even vegetable proteins like soybeans and grains. Hence, we would give an asthmatic child papaya mint tablets or other digestive aids to help improve digestive function.

Lastly, there is one nervine herb in particular that has proven very beneficial for asthmatic children. That herb is lobelia. While there are many who criticize lobelia, saying it is potentially harmful, we have found it to be a most beneficial and harmless remedy. Lobelia is a strong relaxant and deobstruent (meaning it opens obstructions). It relaxes the stomach (a common problem in asthmatic children) and dilates the bronchial passages. Many people have used it to stop asthma attacks in place of inhalants.

Many parents have been able to help their asthmatic children using these sorts of procedures. Asthma, however, is a chronic, not an acute, disease. Therefore, it will take considerable effort over a period of months before the body will really be able to overcome the problem. So be patient and don't give up.

The Kidneys

Children with leg pain, back pain or headaches may have some minor kidney problems. The kidneys are particularly stressed when children are fed a lot of meat and other heavy protein foods. Fresh parsley is an excellent herb for the kidneys, if you can get your children to eat it. Lemon juice is also very beneficial for these organs. We often make fresh lemon or limeade sweetened with pure maple syrup or raw honey during the winter months to make sure we are getting our vitamin C. We feel that natural foods are the best way to get all needed vitamins.

When children have been given lots of antibiotics, they often wind up with urinary infections. Cranberry juice is also an old-time remedy for kidney infections. Unfortunately, most of the cranberry juice you buy commercially is sweetened with sugar. Go to a health food store and buy some that is sweetened with fruit juice.

I have also found that a combination of herbs such as dandelion, marshmallow, cornsilk, cleavers, queen of the meadow, juniper berries, uva ursi or parsley can be very beneficial for the kidneys. This formula may be used in conjunction with minerals and licorice root to stop bedwetting. Uva ursi is an excellent herb for urinary infections. It works best taken as a tea (mix in some peppermint to improve the taste). Kidney herbs can also be used in conjunction with other infection-fighting or immune-building herbs in cases of kidney and bladder infections.

The most important thing you will do for your children's kidneys, however, is to make sure they have PURE water to drink. Children do not like to drink tap water because it is loaded with chlorine and other chemicals. These chemicals are harmful to the body and have been shown in studies to contribute to heart disease and cancer. Hence, the body avoids them as much as possible. Because of this, most Americans wind up consuming large quantities of soda pop, milk, juice and any other beverage except water. However, the kidneys need water in order to be able to filter the impurities out of the body. So, the only way to get pure water is to make it yourself.

Carbon filters are not sufficient to do the job and bottled water may or may not be pure. According to *Organic Gardening*, April '88, "bottled water legally does not have to be any purer than normal tap water." The government's only purpose for regulating "bottled" water is to make sure that the water is no *worse* than tap water. Hence, to properly treat water you must either distill it and then filter it through carbon or you must run it through a high quality reverse-osmosis unit coupled with carbon. Since distillation is expensive and produces flat-tasting water, we have chosen to purchase a reverse osmosis unit. We use the Nature's Spring unit produced by Nature's Sunshine Products because we feel it is one of the best on the market. The water produced by this unit tastes good and children (and yourself) will naturally start drinking more water when you have good-tasting water around. We feel this is a critical part of preventative health care in our family and we wouldn't be without our unit.

Purchasing such a device represents a capital investment, but you'll probably rapidly recover the difference quickly because you'll be spending less money for juice and soda. Plus, you'll prevent a lot of health problems in the future.

Part Five

Infection

nfection is a major concern for most people, because we have been taught that "germs" (i.e., bacteria and viruses) cause disease. However, our belief is that bacteria and viruses attack weakened and diseased tissue, just as flies are attracted to garbage piles and mosquitoes are attracted to swamps. The flies do not cause the garbage piles and the mosquitoes do not cause swamps. One can spray these environments with pesticides to kill the insects, but when the pesticides wear off the insects will return. Furthermore, those vermin which survive the poisoning are those which are most resistant to the poisoning. So, we breed stronger and stronger bugs. The same has been happening with antibiotics.

It has been our observation that the sickest children are often the ones receiving the most medications. Furthermore, the medications do not make them stronger, but actually seem to make them less resistant to disease. Continued use of antibiotics breed stronger and stronger strains of bacteria. It seems that children (and adults) get to the point where their natural resistance is completely gone, so that every time they quit taking antibiotics, within a few weeks they have another (usually worse) infection.

One of the most popular explanations for this problem is that antibiotics kill not only the harmful bacteria, but the friendly bacteria which live in our colon as well. These lactobacillus bacteria actually help to protect our body against harmful bacteria and yeast infections. This is why children who are constantly using antibiotics often wind up with thrush (yeast infection).

We have only given a child an antibiotic once. We gave it to our oldest daughter when she was just one year old because she got an infection in her gums. Fortunately, even though we didn't know how to naturally treat the infection, we did know enough to feed her yogurt with live bacteria cultures to restore the friendly bacteria in the colon. This probably helped us avoid more serious infections in the future. Today, you can get lactobacillus and other friendly intestinal flora in both capsule and powdered form. This can be put into some juice or sprinkled on some food and fed to a child after he has had antibiotics.

However, I think that there are other reasons why antibiotics tend to make the immune system weaker. First of all, antibiotics are poisons. Many children experience side-effects from these drugs. They have been known to kill people. Even the name suggests the toxic nature of these compounds - "anti" means against and "biotic" means life. So, antibiotic means "against life." Think about it.

Furthermore, when we use antibiotics we are trying to do something for the body which the body ought to be doing for itself - fighting the infection. I feel that doing things for the body which it is capable of doing for itself makes the body lazy. Furthermore, as mentioned earlier, antibiotics do not remove the real underlying cause of disease - the waste material which these scavengers feed on.

GARLIC

Fortunately, there are herbs which support the body in its efforts to fight infection and help to remove the underlying cause of the disease. Our favorite herb example is garlic, which, as previously discussed, we use in enemas and in external applications as well as internally. Garlic has been called "nature's penicillin" because it has powerful infection-fighting qualities with no harmful side-effects. (It does have one unpleasant, but harmless side-effect, its smell.)

In his book, *Advanced Treatise in Herbology*, Dr. Edward Shook had this to say about the valuable antibiotic properties of garlic:

> "The use of garlic in the 1st World War [WWI] as an antiseptic was most sensational. In 1916 the British government asked for tons of the bulbs, offering one shilling a pound for as much as could be produced. A great quantity of it was used for the control of suppuration in wounds. The raw juice was expressed, diluted with water, and put on swabs of sterilized sphagnum moss which was applied to the wounds. Where this treatment was given, it has been proved that there has never been one single case of sepsis or septic results. Consequently, the lives of tens of thousands have been saved by this one miraculous herb."

We have used garlic for respiratory problems, earaches, bacterial infections, sore throats, colds, fevers, abscesses and injuries with excellent results. Although children don't like it, we have occasionally given them squirts of garlic oil (garlic oil diluted in olive oil) internally. However, we more frequently use it in an enema, or rub it into the skin over the afflicted area. The volatile oils in garlic (which have the antiseptic action) penetrate right through the skin into the blood and lymph within seconds.

Garlic helps stimulate the flow of blood and lymph, promotes perspiration, expels phlegm and otherwise improves the internal environment to make it unfriendly to harmful micro-organisms. In fact, a nurse who worked in a hospital growing bacterial cultures told me how she had proven to herself the powerful effect of garlic. She took a petri dish with a very powerful strain of bacteria and set a peeled clove of garlic in the center of the dish. Within two hours, every bacteria in the dish was dead. She told me it took eight hours for the strongest antibiotic the hospital had to kill that same strain of bacteria when the antibiotic was sprayed over the whole plate. That shows you how penetrating the effects of garlic are.

TEA TREE OIL

However, garlic is not the only herb which has these powerful abilities. There are many strong-smelling (aromatic) herbs which have antiseptic and antibiotic qualities. These include tea tree oil (or its cousin cajeput), lemon oil, clove oil, thyme oil, pine oil and many others. We use tea tree oil (also known as melaleuca) as a topical antiseptic in our family. Most topical antiseptics (such as iodine, Mercurochrome, etc.) have been shown to damage healthy tissue as well as kill bacteria. Hence, they interfere with and slow the process of healing. This is not true of tea tree oil and many other volatile oils. These products have actually been demonstrated to speed tissue repair and healing while interfering with the growth of harmful microorganisms. Nature's Sunshine's tea tree oil does not sting when applied to nearly all injuries, showing its friendly nature to the skin, so children won't mind applying it themselves. My children will often go get the tea tree oil themselves to apply to a minor injury without my having to encourage them because it does not sting and they sense that it helps.

OTHER INFECTION FIGHTERS

Earlier, I mentioned a blend of cajuput, lemon oil and other oils which I dilute in olive oil and apply externally for infection. We have found this blend to be very effective for infections of many kinds, including tonsillitis, strep throat, mumps, earaches and so forth. Generally, we apply it externally and massage it into the skin with lymphatic massage (see section on pain relief). Even though some of the oils are not considered safe for internal use by the FDA, we will occasionally put a few drops of this oil on the back of the throat to help relieve sinus infection or strep throat. However, remember that volatile oils penetrate rapidly through the skin into the blood and lymph, so this is probably unnecessary.

The combination of echinacea and goldenseal is also very effective. Oregon grape and myrrh gum have properties similar to goldenseal, and we actually prefer these herbs because, unlike goldenseal, they do not affect blood sugar levels. Goldenseal has an insulin-like effect that lowers blood sugar levels and may cause fatigue in hypoglycemics.

We've made various combinations of these herbs into TincTracts™ and glycerites and have found that the glycerine alone is insufficient to mask their bitter taste. However, by adding licorice or stevia, these products can be made palatable. Other herbs to try include: echinacea angustifolia root, echinacea purpurea root, thyme, red clover and yarrow.

Once we learned how to use these kinds of herbs we found it totally unnecessary to use any antibiotics in our family. Furthermore, unlike the antibiotics dispensed by modern medicine, we have observed that the longer children use these herbs the more their natural resistance to disease increases and the less often they are needed.

PART SIX

Pain Relief

ne of the most disturbing things for any parent is to see their child in pain. Unfortunately, like most drugs, pain killers are poisons. They do not remove the cause of the pain; they merely deaden the nervous system so the pain cannot be felt.

Fortunately, there are ways of removing the cause of pain without the use of pain killers. To understand how this is done, we first need to understand the nature of pain—what causes it and how the process can be reversed. We were fortunate enough to learn what causes pain and how to reverse the process while our children were still young. This knowledge was taught to us by C. Samuel West, my other great mentor. These principles are covered in greater detail in his book, *The Golden Seven Plus One*.

UNDERSTANDING PAIN

Our bodies are composed of billions of individual living entities called cells. Each of these cells needs a constant supply of oxygen, nutrients, pure water, heat and a constant removal of the poisonous by-products of metabolism. The cells are supplied with a constant supply of fresh oxygen and nutrients from the circulatory system. A clear fluid which contains dissolved oxygen and nutrients leaves the blood stream to irrigate every cell in the body. This fluid is called lymph.

Some of this lymph is drawn back into the blood stream, carrying with it carbon dioxide and other waste products from the cells. However, much of it is also removed by another system with separate vessels called the lymphatic system.

The lymphatic system is a one-way system which moves the lymph out of the tissue spaces and back into the blood stream. It contains one-way valves to prevent back flow. It also contains lymph nodes which are tiny "sewage treatment" plants to filter the lymph and remove bacteria, toxins, and so forth. The purified lymph is dumped back into the circulatory system at the base of the neck.

The lymphatic system does not have a pump. As the lymph vessels swell with fluid, they contract, which moves some of the fluid. However, lymph flow is greatly increased by movement of any kind. That's why we feel sluggish and sore when we are inactive for long periods. The inactivity causes lymph to pool in the tissue spaces. This slows the exchange of oxygen and nutrients and waste materials which causes the cells to "complain." Moving around, stretching and rubbing sore areas makes us feel better because it pumps the stagnant fluid out of the tissue spaces, helping to bring in fresh lymph laden with oxygen and nutrients.

When cells are damaged in any way (burning, cutting, poisoning, starving, smashing, etc.) they release toxic substances. In turn, these dilate the pores in the small blood vessels. The enlarged capillary pores allow excess fluid to rush into the tissue spaces. This causes fluid to accumulate in the tissues and produce localized swelling. We've all seen this happen with a bump, insect bite or a smashed finger. There is swelling at the site of injury. This swelling creates a stagnant pool which interferes with the flow of oxygen and nutrients and causes an accumulation of toxic waste. The cells complain and we have pain!

RELIEVING PAIN

By understanding this process we can learn how to deliberately prevent and reverse inflammation. When we smash a finger, we instinctively react by grabbing hold of the injured finger and applying pressure. This action prevents leaking fluid from pooling in the tissue spaces to cause swelling. We also yell and perhaps we jump up and down and "dance" a little. These muscular movements increase lymphatic flow and help to drain waste and debris away from the site of injury. The secret is to keep holding on until the pain stops. This usually takes about 5 or 10 minutes. However, in more serious injuries it can take as long as twenty minutes. When the pain stops, you will be able to let go and there will be no more pain.

As parents, we instinctively touch our children when they are hurt. All we need to do is learn to conscientiously apply and direct this loving touch and we can do wonders in helping to relieve minor aches and pains. Whenever a child bumps his head or receives some other similar injury, we should immediately grab the injured spot and apply gentle pressure. Often the children resist the restraint of the pressure, so we switch to another pain relief technique—light, rapid stroking.

This technique involves stroking very lightly and rapidly over the injured area. (There is no pressure applied here; it's like dusting off your clothes.) This movement increases lymphatic flow and rapidly relieves the pain of the injury. With small children, I try to make a game out of it. I say, "Let's brush that nasty pain away, OK?" Then, as I stroke rapidly, I make funny noises to distract the child's attention away from the injury. Usually within a minute or two the child will stop crying, but the stroking should continue for at least five minutes or until the child says the pain has stopped.

It is always important that whenever a child is hurt we do not deny or belittle the pain. Never say, "Big boys don't cry" or "It's only a little cut." Instead say, "That must hurt!" Empathizing with the pain brings dignity to the child and validates his feelings. Children will stop crying faster when we empathize with their hurts than they will if we try to deny them or play them down.

We have used this method to take pain out of smashed fingers, bumps, bruises, and many other minor injuries within minutes. It works incredibly well and yet is so simple and easy to apply.

There are injuries and hurts where the skin may be abraded or burned and where the skin is too sensitive to be touched. In these cases, healing can be aided just by holding your hand over the injured area and imagining that your love is permeating the injury like a warm, healing light OR you can hold your hand about 1-2" above the injured area and do the light, rapid stroking without touching the skin.

These methods work because our body contains electrical currents that generate magnetic fields. These magnetic fields can actually help to move the leaked fluid and protein out of the injured tissues without having to make physical contact. There are many groups that will claim that this ability is limited to those who have had special training under their "guru" or method. However, just about anyone can do this with a little concentration and practice.

We have used these same techniques to relieve headaches, sunburn pain, sore throats, muscle cramps and even earaches. However, with most of these problems, we combine the hands-on technique with the use of herbal remedies. Here are a few examples.

BUMPS AND BRUISES

We have had several instances where this knowledge has come in very handy. In one case, I was with our oldest daughter at a girl scout camp. We had been swimming and while I was changing my clothes, she ran on the wet concrete, slipped and landed on the back of her head. When I got to her, a Red Cross nurse was holding her and she had the biggest goose egg on the back of her head that I have ever seen. I am sure that it was at least 3/4 of an inch tall if not a full inch. Normally I would have applied these techniques immediately, but I was intimidated by the size of the lump and the fact that the nurse was already there. So, I carried her over to the nurse's station.

The head nurse looked at her, went to an ice chest and pulled out a bag of ice. She said, "Hold this on it." Then she went and started to help someone else. I sat there with the bag of ice and thought, "If this is all she is going to do, I can do better." So, I coned the fingers of my right hand and held them as close to the top of the bump as I could without actually touching it. Then I placed my left hand on her forehead. I imagined that with every breath I drew in energy and sent it down my right arm and through the bump to my left hand. It was amazing! The bump actually receded in front of my fingertips and in less than 15 minutes I was massaging the back of her skull, milking out the last of the fluid.

About this time, the nurse came over and said, "I'll get her a Tylenol." I said, "You will not." Indignantly, she responded, "And why not?" "Because," I said firmly, "we don't use drug medications in our family." "Well, she's going to have a splitting headache," she sneered. "She will not," I stated emphatically, "and even if she does, I'll take that away, too."

About two hours later my daughter did complain that it was starting to hurt again. So, I sat down and repeated the technique to remove the swelling and pain. She didn't complain of any pain after that.

Sore Throats

I believe that most sore throats are a result of irritation from sinus drainage. You've probably had the experience of having your upper lip become inflamed (i.e., red and sore) from a runny nose. Well, the same thing can happen to the throat when there is a lot of postnasal drip. These irritated tissues weaken and create an environment for infection, such as strep. The lymph nodes in the throat area become swollen as the excess fluid builds up.

As an adult, I can gargle with various herbs to disinfect the throat area and to encourage flow of blood and lymph. Many people use salt water for this purpose. I prefer a mixture of bayberry rootbark, myrrh gum, goldenseal and capsicum.

Children, however, find it difficult to gargle. Sometimes you can get them to suck on a soothing licorice or slippery elm lozenge, but it is much faster to work with the sore throat as you would any injury. So, I generally apply a mixture of capsicum (or cayenne pepper) extract and lobelia extract directly to the throat. (These are alcohol based extracts as alcohol extracts work best for external applications... glycerites are too sticky.) Then, I gently massage the throat from the top down. This is a very gentle, slow process. Never apply so much pressure that the child feels uncomfortable. Work the sides and the back of the neck as well. You will feel the swollen lymph nodes. The idea is to gently "milk" them until they are no longer swollen. The capsicum and lobelia help to relax the tissues and encourage the flow of blood and lymph.

The first time I tried this was with my oldest daughter. She woke me up in the middle of the night with a "blazing" hot sore throat. She said, "Daddy, it hurts to swallow." I applied the extracts and began to gently massage her throat. Twenty minutes later she said, "Daddy, would you please leave me alone, I want to go back to sleep." That was the end of that incident.

Another time she woke me up with a sore throat when I was just too tired to work on it very hard. I also used garlic oil instead of the capsicum and lobelia, which upset her because she didn't like the smell. Anyway, that time it took me 40 minutes to relieve the pain and get her back to bed.

The last time I worked on a sore throat for her, she woke up in the morning and said, "Dad, I have a sore throat. Make it go away because I want to go to school today." More recently she wanted me to relieve a friend's sore throat which she'd had for three days. For her sore throat she relieved herself by taking some of the glycerites and massaging her own throat. She also knows how to relieve a headache on her own and she's only eleven!

As an alternative to capsicum and lobelia, we often use the blend of cajuput and lemon oils diluted in olive oil. This smells better and is easier to apply. It also makes it easier to do the massage.

HEADACHES

Headaches, of course, are one of the most common types of pain that people take pain killers for. But no one ever cured themselves of headaches by the use of painkillers. The painkillers simply shut down the nerve messages which are telling you that something is wrong.

There are many possible causes of headaches: sour stomachs, constipation, liver problems, a "pinched" nerve or muscle tension. However, whatever the root cause, I find that nearly all headaches involve tension, inflammation and swelling in the neck and shoulder muscles which decreases blood and oxygen flow to the head. As a result, the head complains.

While there are many nervine herbs which may help to relax the body and ease the pain, there are no true pain killers among the herbs. There are anti-inflammatory plants, however. These anti-inflammatory herbs will help to reduce the swelling and inflammation, thus easing the tension and promoting better blood and oxygen flow. The herb we have found works better than any other is white willow bark - especially when it is made as a TincTract™. Other herbs which may be helpful include: wild lettuce, wood betony, feverfew and valerian.

Here again, the fastest way to get rid of a headache is not to take something internally, but to apply something externally and massage the muscles to reduce the swelling and take out the tension. I have only seen a couple of headaches that could not be completely relieved by massaging capsicum and lobelia extract and/or a blend of volatile oils (such as Tei Fu oil or white flower oil) into the neck and shoulders until the muscles became relaxed and flexible.

EARACHES

Parents worry a lot about earaches. First, because they are very painful and second, because they don't want children to lose their hearing. To understand an earache it is important to recognize that it usually has the same root cause as a sore throat. Mucus from the sinuses irritate the eustachian tubes which connect the inner ear and the throat. These tubes allow the air pressure to be equalized on both sides of the eardrum. When these tubes become inflamed due to irritation, they will swell shut. Thus, the flow of blood and lymph must be restored to this tube to reduce the swelling and allow the tube to reopen. As soon as this happens, the ear will stop hurting.

Garlic is one of the very best herbs for this purpose. When we were first married, my wife had some severe ear infections which we had a difficult time getting rid of. Then she discovered garlic. Now, whenever she feels an earache coming on she peels a fresh clove of garlic and puts it in her ear like a hearing aid. (She doesn't put it into the ear canal, she just sets it on the outer part of the ear.) That's it. Within the hour, the pain is gone.

Since children usually won't keep the garlic clove on their ear (unless you tape it in place), we usually use garlic oil. We rub the garlic oil around the ear, especially underneath the ear and jaw moving down into the throat. This encourages lymph flow. Then we put a few drops of warm garlic oil directly into the ear. Make sure the garlic oil is at least body temperature or the coolness of it will cause the ear to contract and increase rather than ease the pain. Rocking or "bouncing" the child also helps to increase lymph flow. I generally give the child a garlic enema as well.

If you don't have garlic handy, try any of the following: lobelia extract, the juice of a baked onion (this works very well), the cajuput and lemon blend mentioned earlier or cinnamon oil. You make cinnamon oil by warming some olive oil with some cinnamon in it and then straining it. I'm sure there are other things that would work as well.

The longest it has taken me to relieve an earache using these methods is four hours. I generally continue to use the garlic oil (or whatever) in the ear for several days following to assure that the problem does not return.

Herbal First Aid for Injuries

In addition to using the lymphatic massage to relieve the pain of injuries, we have also found herbs to be beneficial for these purposes. One of the best of all tissue healing herbs is comfrey. We have soaked injured areas in comfrey tea, taken comfrey internally and applied it in poultices with excellent results. It helps all kinds of tissues, muscles, bones, skin and membranes to heal more rapidly. Once when I had a sore foot I just made up a big tub of comfrey tea and soaked my foot in comfrey tea as hot as I could stand for about 20 minutes. This did the trick, the swelling and pain subsided and did not return. We also make comfrey salve in our family to aid in healing minor abrasions, diaper rash, chapped lips and so forth.

Other herbs that we have found helpful in promoting the healing of injuries include goldenseal, plantain, aloe vera and slippery elm. By mixing these herbs together with a little water to form a paste, you can apply them to a swollen or injured part to ease pain and irritation and promote healing. This is called a poultice. Cover the poultice with a piece of plastic and tape it in place. My favorite combination for a poultice is comfrey, slippery elm and white oak bark moistened with aloe vera juice.

Many herbs can be used for bites and stings. We have also seen lobelia essence, Tei Fu oils, bayberry, plantain, oak leaves and many other herbs completely eliminate the swelling and pain of bee stings and insect bites within minutes. Another great tissue healing herb is aloe vera. The gel is excellent not only for burns and sunburn but for other minor skin irritations as well. Lily of the valley or pine gum will actually draw slivers and infection.

These are just a few of the numerous herbs which can be used for various first aid applications. There are so many possibilities here that it would be pointless to discuss them all. We constantly experiment and are finding new ones.

Part Seven

Emotional Remedies

his book would not be complete without addressing the issue of emotional problems. Like all people, children are most subject to disease when they are under stress. Stress in children, however, is usually caused by stress in their parents. So, if your children seem depressed, easily upset, irritable or otherwise emotionally disturbed, examine yourself. You may need to deal with some of your own emotional stress first. There are many nervine herbs and stress relieving nutritional supplements on the market which you may find helpful.

To relieve nervous stress in children, we developed a children's nervine formula using chamomile, peppermint, catnip and passion flower. These herbs are also good for indigestion and colic, which are usually related to emotional upset. Chamomile is probably one of the very best nervine herbs for children. It aids digestion, expels gas from the bowel, soothes the nerves and reduces inflammation. Catnip and peppermint have similar properties.

We have also had excellent results in helping children with emotional problems by means of flower essences. These are homeopathic preparations made from flowers. The most popular and famous of these are the Bach Flower Remedies. We try to always keep Bach's Rescue Remedy handy in our home. This remedy helps restore calm in an emotional crisis. I've seen Rescue Remedy work miracles in calming a distraught child and we give it to everyone when there is a serious emotional upset.

Here's one of our experiences with this remedy. I came home one day and as soon as I walked in the door our oldest daughter broke into tears. Everybody seemed upset. A neighbor was there holding our youngest daughter. He handed her to me saying, "I'm sorry." Apparently, my wife and children had been visiting his family and he had rolled his truck forward to move it closer to the garage. He hadn't seen our little girl and she had been knocked down and was under the truck. After I reassured him that I wasn't angry, just thankful she was OK, he returned home.

My wife had already given all the children and herself a dose of Rescue Remedy and I gave everyone a second dose. Everyone seemed calmer almost immediately. Then I thought, the person who really needs this is my neighbor, so I took the bottle over to his house. I told him, "you may think I'm strange, but I want you to take some of this." Even though he didn't really believe in herbs, he took some. Later he told me that he felt noticeably better in just a few minutes. That is typical of our experiences with Rescue Remedy.

We have also used flower essences made from North American wildflowers. For instance, the flower essence of chamomile helps promote a sunny, even disposition in children who are upset and distraught. We used it to help mellow the fiesty disposition of one of our children. We also used flower essence of cayenne to help one of our children overcome the tendency to procrastinate. We use flower essences in company with affirmations. We call them flower drops and give them to the child before bedtime with a positive affirmation that helps to promote the change. A source for information and flower essence products may be found in the appendix.

A Divine Stewardship

hildren are a divine stewardship. We believe that our children are really God's children, whom He has entrusted to our care. We believe in our parental intuition. We feel that as parents we know our children better than anyone else. We are better qualified than anyone else to recognize when something is "wrong." We also believe that God can inspire us to find answers for our children's health problems. We do not lightly cast that responsibility onto others, even to well-meaning professionals.

We encourage you to do likewise. You are responsible for your own children, whether you try some of our home remedies or whether you use a professional physician or healer. Make your decisions based on what you feel is best for your family, not on what we say or what others say. That is your right. Don't use any treatment that you don't feel comfortable with, be it herbal or medical.

Several years ago, one of our sons had a problem. At age six, we realized that his testicles had receded back into his body. We asked our midwife to call some of the doctors she knew to ask their opinion of the case. She called a couple of M.D.s, a naturopath and a chiropractor and reported that all of them believed that the only corrective method was surgery. Meanwhile, I had read that most surgeries for undescended testicles wind up causing the testicle to become sterile. I could see little point in this procedure. Some herbalist friends suggested I might try some male hormonal herbs, such as ginseng, but I wasn't sure that was the right approach either.

I prayed and thought deeply about the problem. I also gathered the family around and we all prayed for this son. Finally, a thought came to me. I realized that this son acted very childish for his age. He still used "baby talk" sometimes and often acted very "helpless." I began to feel that his problem was that he was feeling ignored. The "baby" in the family got all the attention, so he had concluded on some subconscious level that the only way to get attention was to go back and be a "baby" again. I decided that this boy needed more fatherly attention. He needed to be encouraged to do more "manly" things and that is exactly what I started to do.

Two months later, my son came to me and whispered, "Dad, let me talk to you." We went into his bedroom and he told me in a low, but excited voice, "Dad, my testicle has descended." We checked and sure enough it had. The next week, while he was taking a bath, I noticed that the other one had descended as well.

This happened without surgery or herbs. It happened because I was willing to follow my parental instincts instead of the advice of others. My boy could have been subjected to costly medical treatments or to a series of fruitless herbal therapies, but instead, some loving fatherly attention, coupled with the faith and prayers of the family had done the trick.

This book has shared with you valuable principles which can help you in the health care of your own family. However, it cannot replace your God-given parental instincts. You must learn what is best for your own family. This book was not designed to teach you how to treat cancer, diabetes or other serious ailments. It was designed to provide you with understanding that will help you with common ailments. If you find your "home remedies" are not working or the problem is serious, you must be wise enough to recognize when you need professional help. However, with experience and faith you will find that those instances where the problem is beyond your experience and ability become farther and farther apart.

There is great satisfaction in having the knowledge to care for your own children. This knowledge has blessed our family. We pray that it will also bless yours.

Making Herbal Preparations

I. INFUSIONS AND DECOCTIONS

The simplist herbal preparations are infusions (teas) and decoctions. An infusion is made by pouring a cup of boiling water over a teaspoon or two of the herb. Then you let the herb steep in the hot water for three to five minutes and strain. This method is suitable for most aromatic (activating) herbs.

A stronger preparation may be made by simmering the herb for 30-40 minutes at a low temperature. Use about two teaspoonfuls of herb per cup of water. Simmer soft parts such as flowers, fruits and leaves for twenty to thirty minutes and harder parts such as roots and barks for thirty to forty minutes, then strain. It is always best to use pure water when making herbal preparations rather than tap water. Both infusions and decoctions may be sweetened with a little raw honey, glycerine or other natural sweetener. Store unused portions in the refrigerator.

II. GLYCERITES

A basic glycerite is made like a decoction, only extraction times are longer. To make a basic glycerite, simmer the herb for two to three hours at a very low temperature. Strain and add an equal amount of glycerine.

Glycerine is available from most drugstores. Just tell the druggist you would like to order a gallon of 99% pure glycerine. (I like the Colgate/Palmolive brand best). Or, you can order pure vegetable glycerine from the sources listed in the back of this book.

This glycerite should keep for several months to several years if you keep it in a sealed container in a cool dark place. The only problem we've ever observed is that it grows mold if you don't get enough glycerine in it for proper preservation.

Another way of making a glycerite is to combine equal parts of glycerine and water and then extract the herb in this mixture as described above. Strain and store as before. Since glycerine helps to extract the herbal constituents, this makes a much stronger (and stronger tasting) herbal preparation.

III. Sealed Simmer Glycerites

Here's how you can make a "sealed simmer" glycerite. You will need to collect the following materials:

1. Canning jars (1/2 pint, pint or quart, depending on how much you want to make) with rings and lids.

2. A pot or pan big enough to hold the jars.

3. Purified water (distilled or run through a reverse osmosis water treatment appliance).

4. Glycerine. Glycerine is available from most drugstores. Just tell the druggist you would like to order a gallon of 99% pure glycerine. (I like the Colgate/Palmolive brand best). Or, you can order pure vegetable glycerine from the sources listed in the back of this book.

5. The herbs you wish to extract. These may be fresh or dried.

Then, you will need to complete the following steps.

1. Wash the jars, rings and lids thoroughly in hot, soapy water and rinse in hot water so they are clean and sterile, just as you would do if you were going to do canning.

2. Place the herbs in the jars. For fresh herbs, you pack the jar full of the herb. With dried herbs you use about one ounce per pint.

3. Fill the jar leaving about 1/2 inch of headroom with a mixture of 60% glycerine and 40% water.

4. Place the jar into the pan and fill the pan about 1/2 up the sides of the jars with water. You can process as many jars as your pan will hold.

5. Simmer the jars in the water for two to three hours. Or, if you are in a hurry, bring the water to boiling and boil the jars for 20-40 minutes. Barks and roots require more processing time than leaves, flowers and fruits.

6. Strain the herbs out of the solution using a clean, fine cotton cloth. The resulting liquid should be put into a bottle with a tight fitting lid and stored in a cool, dark place. It should remain good for about two to three years.

A Guide to Children's Formulas

The following is a guide to children's formulas which can be used in each step of the ABC Herb method outlined in this book. Products are listed in alphabetical order under each category. Products marked with an asterisk (*) were formulated by Steven Horne and/or L. Carl Robinson.

ACTIVATORS

These formulas help to activate the healing energies of the body and are useful for most acute ailments. (see pages 15-18)

Children's Composition Plus*	Limited Edition Herbs
Peppermint and Yarrow*	Tri-Light
Peppermint/Elder/Yarrow Blend	Herbs for Kids
VI Blend	Herbs for Kids

Do-it-yourself Formula (1 part yarrow flowers, 1 part elder flowers and 1 part peppermint)

BUILDERS

The following help to supply trace minerals for building up children's bodies. (see pages 27-29)

Aromin*	Nature's Sunshine Products
Herbal Minerals II*	Limited Edition Herbs

Do-it-yourself Formula (4 parts red raspberry, 2 parts oat straw, 2 parts alfalfa, 1 part nettles and 1 part horsetail)

These formulas help to boost the immune system to prevent illness or to help the body fight infection. They are what I call herbal "vaccines." (see pages 25-26)

Echinacea/Astragalus Blend	Herbs for Kids
Echinacea and Eyebright Blend	Herbs for Kids
Echinacea and Thyme*	Tri-Light
Echinacea for Health*	Limited Edition Herbs

Do-it-yourself Formula (4 parts echinacea root, 2 parts thyme, 1 part licorice, 1 part elderberries)

CLEANSERS

COLON AND DIGESTIVE SYSTEM

The following is a very mild laxative formula suitable for small children. (see pages 37-38)

Kid's Cascara Blend*   Limited Edition Herbs

The following are stronger laxative formulas which may also be used for children.

LB extract   Nature's Sunshine Products
Liqua Lax   Tri-Light

The following are aids for upset stomachs, colic, gas, flu, etc. (see pages 38-39)

Catnip and Fennel   Nature's Sunshine Products
Super Catnip & Fennel Plus*   Limited Edition Herbs
Minty Ginger Blend   Herbs for Kids
Tummy Plus   Tri-Light
Do-it-yourself Formula (1 part catnip and 1 part fennel)

SKIN

The following are blood purifier formulas suitable for children. (see pages 41-42)

BP   Nature's Sunshine Products
Grandma's Tonic*   Limited Edition Herbs
Red Clover Blend   Nature's Sunshine Products
Sarsaparilla and Dandelion   Tri-Light
Do-it-yourself formula (2 parts sarsaparilla, 1 part burdock, 1 part dandelion)

LUNGS

The following are good lymphatic cleansers. (see page 45)

Oregon Grape and Echinacea*   Tri-Light
Red Root and Echinacea   Tri-Light
Red Root Combo*   Limited Edition Herbs
Do-it-yourself Formula
(2 parts red root, 1 part echinacea, 1 part Oregon grape and 1 part elderberries)

The following are good for rubbing on the chest for respiratory congestion. (see pagers 45-46) They also work for swollen lymph nodes (pg. 45), sore throats (pg 62) and earaches. (pg 64)

Cajeput and Lemon Blend*	Limited Edition Herbs
Garlic Oil	Nature's Sunshine Products
Lemon Rub	Tri-Light

The following are good expectorant combinations for clearing respiratory congestion. (see pages 46-48)

ALJ	Nature's Sunshine
Cherry Bark Blend	Herbs for Kids
Horehound Blend	Herbs for Kids
Lungs Plus	Tri-Light
Magnificent Mullein*	Limited Edition Herbs
White Pine and Wild Cherry*	Tri-Light
Wonderful Wild Cherry*	Limited Edition Herbs

Do-it-yourself Formula (2 parts wild cherry bark, 2 parts white pine bark, 1 part elderberries, 1 part licorice, 1 part spikenard or elecampne)

KIDNEYS

The following are good kidney formulas for children. (see page 50)

Dandelion and Cornsilk*	Tri-Light
Juniper Berry Blend*	Limited Edition Herbs

Do-it-yourself Formula (2 parts dandelion, 1 part juniper berries, 1 part cornsilk and 1 part cleavers)

PAIN

The following may be helpful for pain and injuries applied topically. (see pages 57-66)

Cajeput and Lemon Blend*	Limited Edition Herbs
Comfrey/Calendula Salve*	Limited Edition Herbs
First Herbs*	Limited Edition Herbs
Lemon Blend	Tri-Light
Lobelia Essence	Nature's Sunshine Products
Tei-Fu Oils	Nature's Sunshine Products
Willow Garlic Oil	Herbs for Kids

The following may be helpful for mild pain when taken internally. (see pages 48-55)

Feverfew Blend	Herbs for Kids
White Willow and Feverfew	Tri-Light
White Willow Plus*	Limited Edition Herbs

NERVINES

The following are helpful for calming emotionally distressed children. (see pages 67-68)

Calming Chamomile*	Limited Edition Herbs
Chamomile/Skullcap Blend	Herbs for Kids
Five Flower Remedy	Flower Essence Services
Peppermint and Chamomile	Tri-Light
Rescue Remedy	(Health food stores)
Valerian Blend	Herbs for Kids

Do-it-yourself Formula (2 parts chamomile, 2 parts catnip, 1 part passion flower, 1 part peppermint)

Product Sources

Limited Edition Herbs, Inc.
8084 W. McNab Road, Suite 1000
North Lauderdale, FL 33068
1-800-HERB-JOY

This company produces TincTracts™ and the latest versions of many of the formulas mentioned in this book. Although this company is small, it produces some of the most innovative herbal products available anywhere.

Nutritional Resources Inc.
302 E. Winona Ave.
Warsaw, IN 46580
1-800-TOP-SELF

Source for traditional flower remedies and educational materials.

Nature's Sunshine Products, Inc.
P.O. Box 19005
Provo, UT 84605
1-800-435-1422

Nature's Sunshine Products has a broad line of high quality products sold through independent distributors nationwide. You can obtain Tei Fu oil, the Nature's Spring reverse-osmosis water treatment appliance, garlic oil and other products mentioned in this book from this source.

Tri-Light
14618 Tyler Ft. Rd.
Nevada City, CA 95959

Markets herbal products for children in glycerine formulas.

Frontier Herbs Cooperative
Box 299
Norway, IA 52318
1-800-669-3275

You can purchase bulk herbs, essential oils, pure vegetable glycerine and other supplies for making your own children's herb formulas from this cooperative.

Suggested Further Reading

Austin, Phylis, Agatha Thrash, and Calvin Thrash. Natural Healthcare for Your Child. Sunfield: Family Health Publications, 1990.

Christopher, John R. Herbal Home Health Care. Provo: Christopher Publications, 1976.

Finn, Tom. Dangers of Compulsory Immunizations: How to Avoid Them Legally. New Port Richey: Family Fitness Press, 1983.

James, Walene. Immunizations: The Reality Behind the Myth. New York: Bergin & Garvey, 1988.

Kaminski, Patricia. Helping Today's Child: The Magic of Flower Essences. Nevada City: Flower Essence Society, 1989.

Keith, Velma J., and Monteen Gordon. The How to Herb Book. Pleasant Grove: Mayfield Publications, 1984.

Mendelsohn, Robert S. How to Raise a Healthy Child...In Spite of Your Doctor. New York: Ballentine Books, 1984.

"Mothering Special Edition: Immunizations." Mothering Magazine P.O. Box 8410, Santa Fe, NM 87504.

Reed, Barbara. Food, Teens and Behavior. Manitowoc: Natural Press, 198.

Riggs, Maribeth. Natural Child Care. New York: Harmony Books, 1989

Scott, Julian. Natural Medicine for Children. London: Gaia Books, 1990.

Shook, Dr. Edward E. Advanced Treatise in Herbology. Beaumont: Trinity Center Press, 1978.

Smith, Lendon. Feed Your Kids Right. New York: McGraw-Hill, 1988.

Tarr, Katherine. Herbs, Helps, and Pressure Points for Pregnancy and Childbirth. Provo: Sunbeam Publications, 1984.

The Grain and Salt Society. How to Legally Avoid Immunizations of All Kinds. P.O. Box DD, Magalia, CA 95954.

Theis, Barbara, and Peter. The Family Herbal. Rochester: Healing Arts Press, 1989.

Thrash, Agatha, and Calvin. Home Remedies: Hydrotherapy, Massage, Charcoal and other Simple Treatments. Seale: Thrash Publications, 1981.

Thrash, Agatha, and Calvin. Rx Charcoal. New Lifestyle Books, 1988.

Index

L

laryngitis 38
lavender oil 33, 38, 39
leg cramps 27
leg pains 42
lemon Balm 16
lemon juice 42
lemon oil 38, 46, 53
lemon grass 7, 16
licorice 22, 52
licorice root 8, 24, 31
licorice root TincTract™ 10, 24
lily of the valley 55
Liquid Calcium 23
liver problems 53
lobelia 10, 16, 40, 41
lobelia essence 52, 54, 55
lymphatic system 37, 48

M

magnesium 23
magnetic fields 50
malaria 21
manganese 23
marshmallow 8, 42
measles 21, 34, 35
melaleuca 46
menthol 39
Millet, Edward Milo 7
minor abrasions 55
Missouri snakeroot 21
mood swings 23
morning sickness 23
Mowrey, Daniel B. 21
mucilagenous herbs 8, 33
mucus 54
mumps 21, 47
muscle tension 53
mustard powder 7
myrrh gum 8, 22, 38, 47, 52
myrrh oil 38

N

nausea 6, 27, 32
nervine herbs 41, 53
nervines 31
nervous stress 56

O

oak bark 8
oak leaves 55
oatstraw 23, 24
Olbas Cough Syrup 40
oregano 7
Oregon grape 8, 22, 35, 38, 47
organically grown produce 19

P

painkillers 48
pain relief technique 50
papaya enzyme tablets 32
papaya fruit 32
parsley 8, 24, 42
parthenium integrifolium 21
passion flower 56
paste 55
pau d'arco 22
peppermint 7, 14, 15, 23, 28, 30, 32, 38, 56
peppermint soap, Dr. Bonner's 34
phosphorus 23
pimples 6, 27
pine gum 55
pine oil 46
plantain 8, 55
polio 21
post-nasal drip 27
poultice 55
pox 6
prune juice 31

Q

queen of the meadow 42

R

rashes 6, 27
raspberries 8
raspberry leaves 8
red beets 35
red clover 22, 35, 38, 47
red raspberry 23, 24
red root 38
Redmond clay 34
respiratory congestion 6, 15
respiratory problems 45
respiratory tract 27

Other Titles Available through Whitman Books, Inc.

WHITMAN
PUBLICATIONS

302 E. WINONA AVENUE
WARSAW, IN 46580
1-800-421-2401

Nutritional Herbology
By Mark Pedersen

Have you ever wondered which herbs are good sources of iron, chromium, selenium or calcium? Well, this book is for you. Mark Pedersen's Nutritional Herbology is a one-of-a-kind resource book giving you a complete and comprehensive summary of what nutrients are in your herbal supplements and how they work!

You will find detailed nutritional analysis for hundreds of herbs, including Chinese constitutional combinations. With each herb's nutritional profile is an historical summary of the herb's use, a list of medicinal properties, as well as folk remedies.

Nutritional Herbology is an indispensable reference for both the modern herbalist and for those interested in natural remedies. Over four years of extensive research and lab work has gone into bringing you this landmark work!

Nutritional Herbology: A Reference Guide to Herbs is 321 pages, soft bound, 8.5 x11 inches.

Retail $21.95

A Guide to Motherhood: Herbs, Helps & Pressure Points For Pregnancy & Childbirth
By Katherine Tarr

Using herbal remedies and natural techniques, this book contains recommendations and information for a healthy pregnancy and childbirth. Based on the actual experience and observations of a group of Utah lay-midwives, this information has been used to overcome many problems occuring during pregnancy and childbirth.

Although this book focuses on home birth, most of the information can also be used to create a better hospital experience.

A Guide to Motherhood: Herbs, Helps and Pressure Points for Pregnancy and Childbirth by Katherine Tarr is 85 pages, soft bound.

Retail $7.95

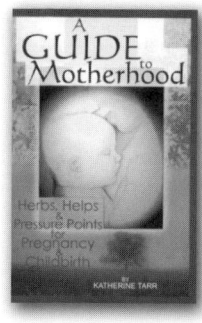

The Family Natural Remedies Guide
By Katherine Tarr

Using herbal remedies and natural techniques, this book contains recommendations and information for maintaining your family's health. Our bodies have the remarkable ability to heal themselves if we just give them the nutrients they need. Here is a convenient A-Z guide to effective remedies to regain and maintain health.

Katherin Tarr has been a midwife for more than twenty years and the owner of a health food store for ten years. This book is the culmination of countless hours of researching and answering people's questions.

The Family Guide to Natural Remedies by Katherine Tarr is 134 pages, soft bound.

Retail $8.75

Ordinary Plants with Extraordinary Powers

Philip Fritchey, MH, ND, CNHP

PRACTICAL HERBALISM
BY PHILIP FRITCHEY, MH, ND, CNHP

Practical Herbalism is destined to become a favorite reference for experienced herbalists and natural health newcomers alike. Drawing on nearly two decades of personal experience, observation, and research, Dr. Fritchey provides a refreshing and enlightening historical perspective, and a bounty of reassuring, down-to-earth methods for using commonly found or easily grown medicinal herbs.

Practical Herbalism will take you on a journey from its "ancient roots" to modern science beginning with the evolution of Herbal Medicine in the West. Learn how the healing salvation of God-given herbs was dragged from common knowledge to "quackery," and how the revival of interest in natural health might have saved thousands of years of herbal wisdom from eradication. Learn simplified processes for gathering, preserving, and making good medicine from everyday plants—techniques once familiar to every self-sufficient household. Learn why and what an herb does is more important than what it is. Then follow along as Dr. Fritchey takes you on an in-depth exploration of 46 very common "Ordinary Plants with Extraordinary Powers." Learn when and how you can use the herbs that can be readily found in your own neighborhood or easily grown in your own garden just as herbalists and wise-women have done for centuries. Compare notes with the ancients, and find validation in current scientific studies. Most of all, find comfort and reassurance in the healing gifts of a Loving Creator which have been placed all around us in anticipation of our every need.

Practical Herbalism: Ordinary Plants with Extraordinary Powers is 444 pages, flexi-bound.

Retail $34.95

THE HOW TO HERB BOOK
BY VELMA KEITH AND MONTEEN GORDON

Written as a "how to" on herbs for yourself and your family, this book gives practical, concise information in an easy-reference form.

The How to Herb Book stresses common, easily available herbs. The remedies used are chosen for effectiveness, ease of use and have been tested by time and experience.

Includes herbs, vitamins, minerals, diets, juice fasts, exercise, pregnancy, babies and much more. An indispensible book designed for quick reading to give confidence and assurance with using herbs.

The How to Herb Book is 256 pages, soft bound.

LET'S REMEDY THE SITUATION
by Velma J. Keith and Monteen Gordon

Retail $13.95
$15.95 Spanish

THE SCIENCE & PRACTICE OF IRIDOLOGY
BY BERNARD JENSEN, DC, ND

This recently reprinted edition written by Dr. Bernard Jensen is a comprehensive and classic treatise and course of instructions on the science of analyzing body ailments by studying the eyes. The 360-page book includes color photos and numerous charts.

The Science & Practice of Iridology is 360 pages, hard bound.

Retail $46.95